ATTITUDE DETERMINES ALTITUDE

WORKBOOK

Elevate Your Mindset and Bring Success to Your Life

DR. KAROCKAS "DOC ROCK" WATKINS

Attitude Determines Altitude Workbook
by Dr. Karockas Watkins
© 2024 by Dr. Karockas Watkins. All rights reserved.

Editing by Adam Colwell's WriteWorks, LLC, Adam Colwell and Ginger Colwell
Cover and interior design by Clarity Designworks
Published by Dr. Karockas Watkins for "Doc Rock" through KDP and IngramSpark
Printed in the United States of America
ISBN (Paperback): 979-8-9914678-5-8

While the author has made every effort to provide accurate internet addresses at the time of publication, neither the publisher nor the author assumes any responsibility for errors or for changes that occur after publication. Further, the publisher does not have any control over and does not assume any responsibility for author or third-party websites or their content.

All accounts from Dr. Karockas Watkins' life experiences are non-fiction. All other stories featured throughout this workbook are ficticious accounts based on actual experiences and events. Any resemblance to real persons or ficticious characters, dead or alive, or other real-life of ficticious entities, past or present, is entirely coincidental.

CONTENTS

RISE TOWARD A GREATER, MORE IMPACTFUL LIFE

Everyone one of us has an attitude. Whether it's good, bad, or something in between, your attitude matters—but I have noticed that many people may not be aware of how their attitude plays a major part in their _____ in life.

Many people suffer from bad attitudes. I know I did. For example, when I was an engineering student at Kettering University, recognized as one of the toughest engineering schools in the country, my mindset was that I was average, while other students had an attitude of high achievement, no matter the cost.

My calculus teacher and mentor, Dr. David Green Jr., challenged me to believe that I could be one of the best. This caused me to begin developing my attitude toward dedication, grit, and success. Dedication means to never give up, no matter how hard it is or how bleak it looks, remaining _____ to the end goal. Grit means to fight, to grind relentlessly with intensity and tenacity. Every morning, I had to have that attitude and walk in it, knowing that grit had to first occur in the mind before it could happen on the field.

Success required fulfilling the mandate and purpose for my life. It was not doing what everyone else was, but what I had been meant to do, seeing it within myself and making it a reality.

Do you have an attitude of dedication and grit? Explain why or why not.

_____

_____

_____

_____

_____

Later, as a young engineer at International Business Machines Corporation (IBM), my attitude was again challenged by an IBM executive, Bob Dubose. He saw potential within me that my mindset had not yet recognized, and he wanted me to aspire to be at the top. I was doing good work, but he stretched me to think and do great work. To be stretched means to open up our minds to believe that we can do more, realizing the _____ inside of us, and seeing ourselves able to advance to a different, higher position. Great work requires putting in the time, energy, and research, after we have stretched ourselves, to get to the desired end goal.

SAM'S STORY

Ever since he was a boy, Sam felt constant pressure to stretch himself, but not for the right reasons. Shy and scholarly, Sam looked up to, and ceaselessly compared himself to, his seemingly carefree and undeniably cool brother, Jensen. Even into their teenage years, Sam never thought he measured up to Jensen's personality or to his brother's expectations of him. However, Sam would later come to realize that the main reason his brother often came across so demanding of him was because Jensen believed he was carrying the load for both them and their mother in a family sorely missing the presence of their father. Their dad had gone missing when they were small and was presumed dead.

As the two boys became young men and together took over the family business that their mother left to them, Sam and Jensen grew closer. Even though they remained stubborn and sometimes combative with each other, the brothers learned how to leverage their different personalities and turn them into strengths as they dealt with one demon after another on the job. Ultimately, they met every challenge, the business went nationwide, and it became both highly sought after and very successful.

Sam also discovered that as he stretched himself for the right reasons—with a belief in himself and in pursuit of his potential—he had a greater impact on others, including his renegade brother. Once, when Jensen was weary and felt like giving up, Sam boldly encouraged him to carry on. "No. No you don't. You don't get to quit. We don't get to quit in this family. This family is all we've ever had."

Questions for application:

1. What challenge do you have to overcome to believe in yourself and pursue your potential? Explain.

_____

_____

_____

_____

_____

2. How has your family helped or hindered your ability to stretch yourself to meet your goals?

_____

_____

_____

_____

_____

3. Describe the most recent time you felt like giving up. What ultimately helped you carry on?

_____

_____

_____

_____

_____

Our attitude is determined by the way we see and handle situations from an emotional and mental _____. Many, for example, view themselves from the stance of being a victim rather than a victor.

I knew a gentleman who always saw himself as a failure. He'd blame others for what they thought about him and appropriate their thoughts as his own. I routinely talked to him about the power of mentally seeing himself as successful. I told him that if he could see his own success on the canvas of his imagination, he could have it. Doing this required forming a mental picture of where he could go, what he could be, or what he could have.

"You cannot have anything that you don't see," I said, "because it is a preview of a coming attraction and of what can possibly happen." I taught him that seeing his success allowed him to then form habits and disciplines to achieve that success. Today, that gentleman is doing well and running his own company that helps others get through life's crises.

Describe how you can begin using your imagination to improve your overall attitude.

_____

_____

_____

_____

Others feel their attitude is expressed emotionally by getting sad or mad in certain situations, but our attitude is _____ than emotions and _____ than merely feeling down, angry, or frustrated. It's about how we see our lives, our goals, and our expectations when they are not being fulfilled. What we call depression or anger is really our attitude about our perceptions of what we have done or what we can do in the future. It's about whether we have control of those things, experience shortfalls, or are on target. The real issue is looking at what we have or have not accomplished in comparison to what we want to accomplish.

Compare what you have or have not accomplished to what you want to achieve. What does that tell you about yourself?

_____

_____

_____

_____

_____

Once, I was very frustrated at where I was in my professional life. I felt that I had worked as hard as or harder than others, yet they seemed to be doing better than I was. I was playing a comparison game that I could not win. The more I looked at others, the angrier I got.

It wasn't until I changed my attitude about working, believing, and trusting in my own place and space that I gained any peace. I had to look at myself, and what I was doing, thinking, and saying, to understand that I wasn't trying to achieve or become what someone else was. I needed to _____ on using my own talents, gifts, and passions and nothing more. I had to learn to be comfortable that the place I'd achieved and the space I'd occupied was exactly where I was supposed to be, even if the grass seemed greener on the other side. That allowed me to flourish.

DEAN'S STORY

Being comfortable in both his place and his space was never easy for Dean. One reason for that was an unrelenting feeling that he needed to compete with his business partner, Jared. The pest control company they ran together came with constant challenges and headaches, but Dean believed Jared had better business sense than he did, and he didn't like that. His perceived shortcomings made him angry. So, Dean questioned Jared and argued with him at every turn. Sometimes, Dean felt it should be his place to control the business outright; other times, he was convinced his space should be elsewhere entirely. More than once, Dean considered quitting and starting his own extermination operation.

What turned things around? Dean realized that his anger wasn't with Jared, but with himself. Despite his outward bravado, Dean was very insecure. Once he admitted that to himself and got help to work on his self-esteem, his mindset changed—and it showed in his attitude. Instead of competing with Jared, Dean decided to become the best business partner he could be. He discovered and elevated the strengths already present in his personality and abilities, and he brought them to the table to complement Jared's temperament and talents.

In no time, their pest control business was thriving, and so was their relationship. As the duo began to flourish, Dean philosophized, "The universe is trying to tell us something we both should already know. We're stronger together than apart."

Questions for application:

1. Dean discovered his proper place and space by looking within. How would you describe your professional place and space right now?

   Place:

   _____

   _____

   _____

   _____

   _____

   Space:

   _____

   _____

   _____

   _____

   _____

2. Are you satisfied with those? Why or why not?

   _____

   _____

   _____

   _____

   _____

3. How can you begin to change your mindset in these areas so that you can gain peace professionally and personally?

_____

_____

_____

_____

_____

Theodore Roosevelt, our nation's twenty-sixth president, rightly and famously said, "Comparison is the thief of joy." If we are going to judge ourselves, our actions, or where we are at any given point, we do not need to compare ourselves to others. We judge according to what we know, who we know we are, and what we know we can do—and all of that is informed by what we are _____ to do and be.

In 1884, a young man died, and after the funeral, his grieving parents felt they should establish a memorial to their son. Determined and confident in who they were and what they could do, they met the president of Harvard University. After they expressed their desire to fund a memorial, the college president dismissed their request. "Perhaps you have in mind a scholarship instead?"

"No," the mother replied, "we were thinking of something more substantial than that—perhaps a building."

The president of Harvard brushed aside the idea as being too expensive, and the couple departed. It wasn't until the following year that the beleaguered president learned that the couple had gone west and established a then-massively priced $26 million memorial they named Leland Stanford Junior University—better known today as Stanford University.[1] Their undaunted attitude certainly paid off in honoring their son with an enduring legacy.

What you are meant to *do* and *be* informs your legacy.

1. What professional legacy do you want to have?

_____

_____

_____

_____

_____

2. What personal legacy do you want to have?

_____

_____

_____

_____

_____

Attitude thrives off of a positive _____ fed by a proper perspective, and lots of people seemingly want to be on top, successful, and in control. But they'll never get there when their mindset is on the bottom. Perhaps they don't want to work hard, failing to understand the many sacrifices that must happen in order to be on top. It could be that they accept failure as final, so that mindset keeps them thinking like someone at the bottom who is unsuccessful in fulfilling their goals, missions, and dreams in life.

Joe Theismann enjoyed an illustrious career as quarterback of the Washington Redskins (today's Washington Commanders). He led the team to two Super Bowl appearances, winning in 1983 before losing the following year. When an infamous leg injury, incurred during a nationally-televised game in 1985, forced him out of football, he was Washington's all-time leading passer. However, Theismann had a confession about the season after winning his first and only Super Bowl title.

"I got stagnant," he admitted. "I thought the team revolved around me. I should have known it was time to go when I didn't care whether or not a pass hit (wide receiver) Art Monk in the '8' or the '1' on his uniform. My approach had changed. I was gripping about the weather, my shoes, practice times—everything."

He then said, "Today I wear my two rings—the winner's ring from Super Bowl XVII and the loser's ring from Super Bowl XVIII. The difference between those two rings lies in applying oneself and not accepting anything but the best."[2] What happened? His mindset had regressed from the top to the bottom, and it ultimately made him less successful.

Right now, is your mindset closer to the top or the bottom? Why?

_____

_____

_____

_____

_____

Complacency is a blight that saps your energy, causes a drain on your brain, and dulls your attitude. The first symptom is satisfaction with things as they are. The second is the rejection of things as they might be. "Good enough" becomes today's watchword and tomorrow's _____ in your life. Complacency makes people fear the unknown, mistrust the untried, and abhor the new. Like water, complacent people follow the easiest course: downhill. They draw false strength from looking back.[3]

In other words, they do not challenge themselves intellectually to the point where they change their mindset. They are not open to expect or to do something differently. They are willing to receive and get what they can out of an experience, but they don't have the proper attitude that thinks about how they can take what they are seeing to move toward success or give back to others.

A great attitude is a mentality that is put into action.

CHARLIE'S STORY

As a member of a socially disenfranchised community, Charlie has always had to put her mentality into action to overcome the negative words and actions said or done to her by those who oppose her or her views. This often leaves her mentally and emotionally weary, and that tiredness can easily transform into complacency—manifested by a strong sense of security in who she is, but one that also dangerously prevents her from wanting to continue challenging the social status quo or of envisioning how things might be if she and others in her community were treated better by others.

Charlie has offset her complacency by first facing her fears of gracefully but honestly confronting those who speak or act against her. Next, she has decided to trust that doing this will make a positive impact on her even if it does not change the opinions or actions of those she confronts. Finally, Charlie has decided to choose optimism over pessimism when she thinks about the future. Social evolution, she reminds herself, happens slowly and often haphazardly, but the main thing is to stay true to who she is, and the rest will take care of itself.

"At no point am I threatened any longer by people who question who I am, why I like the things I do, or my legitimacy," Charlie said. "I know who I am very strongly, and I think that's what having and maintaining the right attitude has given me."

Questions for application:

1. What social perception challenge have you had to face personally or professionally?

_____

_____

_____

_____

_____

2. Did it make you complacent? If so, how? If not, how has it negatively impacted you?

_____

_____

_____

_____

_____

3. List three things you can begin doing to confront that challenge with grace and honesty.

   a. _____

   _____

   b. _____

   _____

   c. _____

   _____

In the end, your attitude is in direct proportion to your *altitude.* Swiss psychiatrist and balloonist, Bertrand Piccard, became the first person, along with colleague Brian Jones, to complete a non-stop balloon flight around the globe. Piccard was quoted in National Geographic about the similarity he sees between balloon flight and daily life.

"In the balloon, you are prisoners of the wind, and you go only in the direction of the wind," he said. "In life, people think they are prisoners of circumstance. But in the balloon, as in life, you can change altitude, and when you change altitude, you change direction. You are not a prisoner anymore."[4]

1. What life circumstance is holding you prisoner right now?

   _____

   _____

   _____

   _____

   _____

2. List two ways you can change your altitude about that circumstance so that your attitude will be lifted.

   a. _____

   _____

   b. _____

   _____

Our attitude changes our altitude and dictates our _____. If I have an attitude that I won't be the best, that will drive me not to be promoted, go higher in my field, or create something new. I cannot go any higher than what I am thinking. On the flip side, if I am living in the projects, but I can see myself owning a home, driving a nice car, and doing things that others may not be able to do, my attitude will drive me to do whatever is necessary to achieve those goals.

That's what I did. Even though I was in a situation that may not have been favorable, my attitude allowed me to change my altitude and rise toward a greater, more impactful life.

How we choose to think—our mindset—will not only affect what we expect from life, but it'll impact what we do in life.

I wrote *Attitude Determines Altitude* to encourage those who are pursuing life with the proper attitude, and to transform those who have been struggling with having the proper and necessary attitude to succeed. After completing this workbook, I hope your mind will think and your mouth will say, "Bring it on, world! I can do it!"

Rise Toward a Greater, More Impactful Life **Fill-in-the-Blank Answer Key:**

success	more	mindset
committed	deeper	standard
excellence	focus	outlook
perspective	meant	

1

ATTITUDE DEFINED

*An attitude continually transformed by your mindset
will bring success to your life.*

You are where you are today based on the attitudes you had in the past, and who you will be in the future is based on the attitudes you have today. Better stated, you are today what you thought yesterday, and you will be tomorrow what you are thinking today.

Your attitude _____ your success and failure—and it is time for it to give you more success.

Success, however, is not just the acquisition of material things or professional status. *Success is the accomplishment of an aim or purpose.* I discovered this to be true when I saw myself gaining some things that I never had but still being unfulfilled. It felt good in the moment, but there was no longevity to that feeling.

As I asked myself, *What is this?* I realized that _____ comes when we achieve or accomplish who we are called to be on this earth.

I believe every person has the right to a successful life.

1. How have you defined success up to this moment?

_____

_____

_____

_____

_____

2. How has that definition changed based on what you just learned?

_____

_____

_____

_____

_____

This requires you to discover your "why." It is the reason you exist, your purpose for living. Until you figure it out, you'll always think about the "how" and the "when," but never realize them.

Many times, our why is born from our gifts, talents, and struggles, and it is perhaps best seen as that one thing, if we had all the money in the world, that we would do for free. I tell people that their why is that thing that will get them out of the bed when everyone else is still hitting the snooze button.

When we discover our why, we will search diligently to recognize how to accomplish it, and we will wait as long as it takes to gain the knowledge, stability, and experience to fulfill it. Then, the question of when our why happens is swallowed up in the _____ of understanding it.

When I work with clients to help them discover their why, I teach them that their why shouldn't be something that is done just for money, because when they find out what they are meant to do, they'll never "work" a day in their lives. Living out their why will require work and lots of it, but it won't feel like work.

Therefore, if they are complaining about what they do, are stressed out about it, or simply don't want to do it any longer, it wasn't their why to begin with. Their why, instead, will be based on their passion, and it will feed their commitment to it over the long haul.

RON'S STORY

With a doctorate in linguistics, a degree in finance, and an interest in world history, Ron took that pedigree, and his mastery of no fewer than five languages, to become a successful philanthropist, running his own charitable organization. Its various outreaches benefited countries throughout the world, and Ron's added abilities as a leader made him a coveted business consultant. His professional success was evident.

But when Ron discovered his why, it was uniquely personal. Encouraged and mentored by his lifelong friend, Arvin, Ron pursued spiritual enlightenment with a fervor. As his passion for God developed and grew, his earnest faith and zeal automatically infected his professional responsibilities in many affirmative and constructive ways. Confidence in his own immortality infused each one of his earthly domains, and many more lives were changed as a result. "My faith has filled a hole in my heart," Ron said. "It is central to my very existence. It's who I am."

Ron's why has shifted him to a more positive place—one where he can be continually transformed by his mindset—because he knows his purpose and has that thing in front of him that drives his emotions to be stable and to grow.

Questions for application:

1. As it was with Ron, religion can be just one positive breeding ground for your why. What other sources can or have influenced the reason you exist and your purpose for living?

_____

_____

_____

_____

_____

2. What are the possible pitfalls of pursuing a why solely for monetary gain?

_____

_____

_____

_____

_____

3. Can you define your why right now? If so, list it here. If not, what can you do to begin identifying your unique why?

_____

_____

_____

_____

_____

Times past

Growing up in government housing in a small town in Alabama, I didn't see many people who knew their why or had an attitude of success. What I did see were attitudes of tradition and mediocrity that were rooted in survival.

I was a church kid, and I loved going to church. Later as a boy, I'd travel with my stepfather, Dr. George Franklin, as he went and preached in country churches. Everyone from my family to my friends religiously went to church, but I didn't see anything that showed me they were really focusing on an attitude of success. Church was just something they did on Sunday, but after that, they went back to the same old mindset of survival.

They had the attitude that good existed, but they were not _____ that good in their lives.

I reasoned, *I don't want to be a part of that.*

With mediocrity, I saw people who were average. My definition of average is to be "on top of the bottom," and that's all everyone wanted. They didn't want to get all the way to the very top. I'd hear, "I'm gonna work, but I'm not going to go overboard," or, "I'm not going to extend myself in order to be my best."

But I don't want to be better than anyone else, I believed. *I want to be the best Karockas I can be. They settle. They're comfortable.*

I want to be more.

Be honest. Are you more prone to settle for mediocrity or do you strive to be more? Why?

_____

_____

_____

_____

_____

I'm thankful I was able to see beyond what was shown to me so that I could envision goodness and success for my life. This happened in a simple yet incredible way when I was just seven years old.

Every summer, I stayed with my biological father's mother, Mama Sally, while my mother and stepfather spent more time with my two younger siblings, Brandon and Ashia. Mama Sally lived across town from where we did, only 15 minutes away, but her home was in the older projects while mine was in a government-assisted home that, while in slightly better condition, was still project housing. My biological father and I often went fishing during those summers, and Mama Sally usually joined us on those hot, summer mornings out on the Tennessee River.

My Mama Sally and I were very close. Even as a boy, I admired her hard work and entrepreneurship. She made Bee-Bops, Kool-Aid that is mixed and then frozen in cups, and sold them, along with pickled eggs, pickled bologna, homemade chocolate and vanilla cupcakes, and Little Debbie cakes to kids and adults in the neighborhood. I helped her shop during the week, and I assisted as she cleaned up the house, all of which brought us together.

As I did each evening, I was sitting at the table by the open window in her small, beige-painted kitchen, hoping to catch a breeze to cool the humidity that still pressed in even after the sun was setting. In the waning light, I could see the outline of the clotheslines against the darkening sky and the silhouette of the barrel grill in the small backyard.

One particular night, I watched as Mama Sally made watermelon flavored Bee-Bops. She was very neat, so the only things out were what she needed at the moment: Kool-Aid, a jug, and a lot of white, pure cane sugar. It smelled so good! She often let me sample a spoonful to see if it was sweet enough.

Mama Sally put them in the freezer that covered one entire wall of the kitchen, and when she went into another room to do something else—I had an epiphany. It was as though God Himself sat down across from me at the kitchen table to have a conversation.

"You have favor on your life. You are going to do great things to literally touch the world. Not just in Alabama, but in the world. So, walk in a place of discipline to get good grades and do what is right. Don't fear any other people of different races or in different cultures. One is no better than the other. They are all different, and you are going to be used in their lives in a special way."

That moment was incredible and so real that I remember it today in such rich detail.

Share a detailed childhood story that had a positive effect on your outlook on life. Conclude with why that moment was so positive for you.

_____

_____

_____

_____

_____

Prior to that night, my attitude was that of a loser and a failure. I looked at my physical, social, and economic conditions as if they were what *I* was. Physically, I was smaller, slower, and uncoordinated compared to all the other boys who were good in sports. I was the cream puff, always the last person to get picked for the team. Socially, I was a little awkward. I liked reading, fishing, and being around older people and listening to them, so I was different than most of the guys around me. They were getting into trouble, and I wasn't. Economically, we lived in the projects. My mother and stepfather worked, but we just didn't have what most everybody else did. I thought we were not successful, and I knew I didn't want to live in subsidized housing when I was older.

Most people are _____ of their environment, but they can even be from a decent physical environment and still have no hope. But when I heard those words in my heart and mind about favor and the great things I was going to do, they addressed my physical, social, and economic conditions. They let me know that I was not a loser. I was not a failure. I had _____ within me. I had been given a vision that I would work with people of other races to achieve greatness.

WILL'S STORY

As a reporter for a major daily newspaper, Will constantly had to battle a sense of failure. Every day, he would work on the assignment given to him by his editor, not knowing if his article would make the final cut for the next edition. Sometimes it did, periodically with placement on the front page of the section, but more often than he liked, it didn't. At those times, Will felt like his research and wordsmithing was all for naught. In the competitive and uncertain environment of the newsroom, Will had to consistently stay confident in his abilities as a writer so that he didn't become either a product or a casualty of that environment.

Then Will investigated and uncovered the existence of a covert, rogue government agency. Not only did the story land his byline on the front page, but it also resulted in inquiries from other publishers. They recognized the greatness Will only dared to believe he possessed as a reporter, and he would go on to become a successful online writer with thousands of credits to his name.

"This is what I believe to be true," Will said. "You have to do everything you can. You have to work your hardest. And if you do, if you stay positive, then you have a shot at living out your greatness."

Questions for application:

1. How do you believe you are a product of your environment, be it from your past or in your present?

_____

_____

_____

_____

2. What can you do to take that knowledge and use it to work against your perceived failures or shortcomings?

_____

_____

_____

_____

_____

3. What do you dare to believe about yourself that can propel you toward achieving the greatness within you?

_____

_____

_____

_____

_____

My attitude began to change, and as it did, so did my life. I went from making failing scores in the first grade to being one of the top students in my elementary school. In fifth grade, Miss Pat O'Shield pushed me so that when I was in middle school, I wanted to be the best. My seventh-grade teacher, Miss Constantine Pope, pushed me even further. Neither one let me _____ for being lowly. They had me thinking that I was the best and that I could achieve and *be* the best. That carried me successfully through high school, earning me a sponsorship with the General Motors Company to attend what was then the GMI Engineering and Management Institute (now Kettering University) in Flint, Michigan.

There, my attitude on life was challenged once again. It came in a most unexpected way from my college roommate, Michael Harris. He was making A's in his engineering classes while I was making B's. One morning at our apartment, I asked him to come to church with me. I was scheduled to preach the 11:00 a.m. Sunday morning message for the first time ever, and I was very excited about the opportunity.

Always unapologetic, he was not at all hesitant to respond.

"You want to go preach and do all the Bible says you can do and all that," he said, "but you don't believe it yourself because I make A's and you make B's, and you are just as intelligent as I am. You don't have confidence, so I'm not going to listen to you. Until your grades reflect what you are saying, I don't want to hear you."

Michael's candor made me mad—yet all the way to church, I was thinking, *He is right.*

Michael boldly and honestly challenged me to assess my self-confidence. Who can you encourage in the same way? Write their name here—and detail what you will say to them.

_____

_____

_____

_____

_____

As I calmed down, I began to consider what I needed to do to change. Not surprisingly, it began with my mindset. I had to start _____ things differently. I realized that I thought I had arrived when, in reality, I hadn't. *I've got to work on this. I can make A's. Why am I not making A's? What is stopping me from being my best?*

I am grateful Michael boldly challenged me to change my mindset and take my attitude to a higher place. I graduated with a mechanical engineering degree and earned honors on my thesis because of that transformation and elevation of my attitude, and I now have a master's degree, two doctorates, and a certificate in business excellence. I own a leadership consulting company, I am chief executive officer of a leading nonprofit business, and I am on a team of cultural leadership consultants with a major insurance broker where I travel, teach, and train others around the world.

My why—to empower, lead, and teach people to reach their goals by helping them to maximize their potential—is being fulfilled.

JENNIFER'S STORY

Just as I had to navigate physical, social, and economic conditions, then ignite my own self-confidence to propel myself forward to achieve my why, Jennifer had to overcome significant personal trauma to attain hers. Two unexpected deaths, first of her fiancé and later of her best friend, preceded revelations about her mother that resulted in her being estranged from many members of her family and friends. Only the constant presence of her father helped her through the loss and pain as Jennifer completed college and went to work at a corporate bank as an analyst.

Intelligent, determined, and strong mentally and physically, Jennifer wanted nothing more than to have a normal adult life, one with stability where she could trust people without question. Part of that process was determining her why. While she enjoyed her work at the bank, Jennifer discovered that her why was to have her own family. She wanted to be a mother different than her own and to find a lifelong companion who had the best qualities of her father and would love her unquestionably.

That's a tall order for any woman regardless of personal backstory—but Jennifer eventually accomplished it, marrying André and having two children, a daughter and a son. They named the boy after her father. "I know I've lived a charmed, beautiful life," she said at her tenth wedding anniversary celebration. "Beauty comes from a life well lived."

Questions for application:

1. Briefly describe a personal trauma you've had to deal with.

   _____

   _____

   _____

   _____

   _____

2. How has that trauma influenced the determination of your purpose for living?

   _____

   _____

   _____

   _____

   _____

3. What's the first thought that came to mind when you read Jennifer's words, "Beauty comes from a life well lived?"

   _____

   _____

   _____

   _____

   _____

Attitude and philosophy

I believe millions of people fall short of the best for their lives because of a lack of excellence in their attitude or personal philosophy of success and growth.

Philosophy is derived from two words: philo-, meaning "to love," and -osophy, meaning "to think." So, our philosophy is simply "loving the way we think." That philosophy has been _____ by our history, the direct and indirect teachings we've received, our financial and social status, and other influences.

Chinese philosopher, Zeng Shen, was young enough to be Confucius' grandson, yet he won high praise from Confucius himself and later taught Zisi, the grandson of Confucius. One of Zeng Shen's famous philosophies goes as follows: "Every day I ask myself three questions. The first is, 'Have I sinned in my thoughts and actions toward others?' The second is, 'Have I broken faith in any of my friendships?' The third is, 'Have I tried to teach anything to others I have not fully learned and understood myself?'"

Not only is each of the three questions extremely important in themselves, but the practice of examining one's own behavior every day is a habit that every person should cultivate.[5]

Life and peace come when we have an attitude where we are careful to check what we are saying, doing, and hearing in every area of our lives.

Ask and honestly answer the following:

1. Have I sinned in my thoughts and actions toward others? If not, how did you avoid it? If so, in what way?

    _____

    _____

    _____

    _____

    _____

2. Have I broken faith in any of my friendships? If not, how did you avoid it? If so, in what way?

    _____

    _____

    _____

    _____

    _____

3. Have I tried to teach anything to others I have not fully learned and understood myself? If not, why didn't you? If so, in what way?

_____

_____

_____

_____

_____

A person's mental attitude has an almost unbelievable effect on both physical and psychological ability. The British psychiatrist, J.A. Hadfield, provided a striking illustration of this fact in his booklet, The Psychology of Power. "I asked three people," he wrote, "to submit themselves to test the effect of mental suggestion on their strength, which was measured by gripping a dynamometer." He set up three different conditions in which they were to grip the dynamometer with all their strength. First, he tested them under normal conditions. The average grip was 101 pounds. Next, he tested them after he had hypnotized them and told them that they were very weak. Their average grip dramatically decreased to only 29 pounds. In the third test, Dr. Hadfield told them under hypnosis that they were very strong. Their average grip jumped to 142 pounds.[6]

Attitude, then, is the mental _____ that causes us to comprehend, see, and handle situations and circumstances in a certain way. It can be seen as the glasses through which we see the world. It controls the choices we make, the opportunities we pursue, the money we earn, and the success we achieve.

1. On a scale of 1-10 (with 10 being the highest), how do you rate the strength of your overall mental attitude?

_____

2. Why did you give yourself that score?

_____

_____

_____

_____

_____

Attitude even plays a significant role in how we read, meditate, and perform. If we don't have the right attitude when we read, it is easy to criticize what we are reading, finding something wrong with every little thing that we consume. If we read with a positive attitude, though, we'll view it from a _____ standpoint. We'll find something, that one good nugget, that will help us go forward with our goals, dreams, and pursuits in life.

When I first read *Emotional Intelligence 2.0*, coauthored by Travis Bradbury and Jean Greaves, I had a negative attitude about the notion that someone's emotional intelligence (EQ) was what made them successful as opposed to their IQ, or intelligence quotient. I thought good old-fashioned smarts was most important. But as I opened myself up and viewed the subject of EQ through the lens of research, I quickly saw that EQ was both positive and beneficial. Not only did I go on to learn more about emotional intelligence, but I also became certified to facilitate EQ seminars, which I've now done around the world. Later, I have dedicated an entire section of this book to how EQ ties with having an attitude that determines your altitude.

Name something you recently read that helped your mental or emotional attitude, and describe how it benefited you and why.

_____

_____

_____

_____

_____

Meditation is where verbalization, visualization, and internalization are used to focus our thoughts to see and rehearse the actions we want. These three forms of meditation encompass and address the basic components of an experience shaped by words spoken out loud, emotions felt as real, and images seen on the canvas of the imagination. If we don't have the right attitude when we meditate, we can be very judgmental of ourselves and others, all "woe is me" and venting in nature. Meditation cannot be done out of rote ritual, or just to see if we will get what we want. Instead, meditation should be done with an attitude of seeking more peace of mind and insight about what we can have and what is in store for us in the _____. That's when our meditations become more dynamic and effectual as we start to see them come to fruition.

MIA'S STORY

Mia certainly had to practice mindfulness as a young woman after learning from her father that her mother was not who she thought it was, but that Mia was actually the product of an affair her father had while he was with the woman who raised her. It was a shocking revelation that caused Mia to question everything she believed about herself and her family. Her therapist recommended self-talk and meditation as techniques that could help Mia cope with her feelings about her fractured past and discover who she truly was as an individual apart from her parentage.

The practice of mindfulness elevated Mia's thinking and enabled her to recognize and nurture her own self-identity. Along the way, she even located and began a friendship with her half-sister, Nadia, in Argentina. Mia ultimately immigrated to that country to live near Nadia in Buenos Aires and become a beloved aunt to her half-sister's son, Milo.

"Speaking and thinking truth about myself changed my life, but finding myself was just the beginning," Mia said. "Having a relationship with Nadia and helping raise Milo has completed the healing of the brokenness from my past and has positioned me to look ahead to a brighter future."

Questions for application:

1. In the past week, what have you said internally about yourself?

_____

_____

_____

_____

_____

2. Was that self-talk positive, negative, or neutral—and what does it make you think of yourself at this moment?

_____

_____

_____

_____

_____

3. Write down how you can start to use meditation and mindfulness to recognize and nurture your self-identity and better define your overall attitude.

_____

_____

_____

_____

_____

In addition, many people have gifts, degrees, and skills, but the reason they don't achieve their life goals is because they don't have a _____ mental attitude about things such as their self-image. Years ago, there was a company that received a less than acceptable grade in their annual certification audit. The organization had talented individuals and a good management staff, but they were focused more on their skill sets than their mindsets.

Top leadership challenged everyone to go from "good to great," using the book of the same name by Jim Collins. Changes were implemented in operations, policies and procedures, and overall work culture. As a result, the staff's mindset was elevated, and they became a unified team that was more productive and efficient. The next audit confirmed a 100-percent improvement in all facets of the company.

1. Share how a recent challenge at your workplace has impacted your self-image as an employee.

_____

_____

_____

_____

_____

2. What did you learn from the experience?

_____

_____

_____

_____

_____

Finally, contrary to what many people may assume, attitude is not always vocal or loud. It can be _____ but have loud results. I was involved in a situation with a city Chamber of Commerce where it wanted to take on a greater role when it came to diversity and equity in the community's culture. A lot of chamber members were opinionated about what we should do, how we should do it, and who should do it. But my attitude was to assess what was going on, view what we needed to do from the standpoint of the chamber's overall mission, and determine how I could help achieve that.

As a result, without being the loudest person in the room, I became the chairman of the diversity, equity, and inclusion task force, and some very positive things have resulted from that role.

1. On a scale of 1-10 (with 10 being the highest), how do you rate your attitude and desire to be an influencer similar to how I was as a member of the chamber?

   _____

2. Why did you give yourself that score?

   _____

   _____

   _____

   _____

   _____

Attitude and how our mind functions

In the Hebrew language, the word "heart" is interpreted as being the center of human thought and spiritual life. We tend to look at the heart as being the seat of our emotions, but in ancient cultures, the heart was also the seat of intelligence. The mind and heart, therefore, are one in the sense of *thought*.

I believe humans are tripartite in nature. Each one of us is composed of body, soul, and spirit. Our bodies are temporal. Our spirits are eternal. Our souls are the place where our mind resides—and our mind can be broken up into three compartments: the conscious, the subconscious, and our conscience. All three are involved in transforming our mindset to change the altitude of our attitude.

Let's look at each one.

The conscious mind is where our purposeful thoughts, as well as our initial reasoning and logical thinking, take place.

How conscious are you of your thoughts as you go through a typical day? Why?

_____

_____

_____

_____

_____

The subconscious mind is the autopilot of the conscious mind and has the responsibility to automatically carry out the finished work of the conscious mind. When our conscious mind has accepted certain norms and values as truth, it is then the subconscious mind that takes that thought and handles our decision-making so that the conscious mind is freed up to receive and process new data.

Do you believe your subconscious mind tends to work for or against your attitude? Why?

_____

_____

_____

_____

_____

Our conscience is our belief system containing ethical and moral principles that control or inhibit our actions or thoughts according to our sense of right or wrong. In order for us to become successful people, our conscience must be transformed. This requires a disciplined process of applying new truths to our lives. These new truths are learned from our beliefs and our experiences. They can also come from workbooks such as this one, credible authority figures, and seminars that are not contradictory to our beliefs.

Where does your belief system originate—and how consistently do you think that system directly affects your thoughts, decisions, and actions?

_____

_____

_____

_____

_____

To prepare our heart and mind to have an elevated attitude, we must continually make three essential decisions.

1. We must die to self.

This concept mandates that we lose sight of our own interests, forget them entirely, and place the interests of _____ first. This positions us to deny our own selfish ambitions. That doesn't mean we cannot have goals, but it does mean those goals must be aligned with what benefits others, not just something we desire.

As a boy, I had always wanted to be a medical doctor. I would read my mom's nursing books, and I took all the science classes I could in high school. One day, while I was contemplating how to get into and pay for medical school, I visited a doctor. He was my mother's colleague, so I knew he would be a great person to give some good advice and serve as a sounding board for my goals.

He explained that he became a doctor because he felt God had "called" him to go into that field. Furthermore, he said his practice was successful because he was doing what God wanted him to do. He counseled me to do the same, and if the medical field was where I was supposed to be, I'd know it. The doctor was aware of my grades and my capabilities, but he told me to return to him for help becoming a doctor only after I knew for sure that was my future direction.

Let me tell you, I had to do some dying to self after that conversation. I knew what I had heard when I was a boy about the favor that was on my life. I just had to confirm my path.

I never made it back to that doctor—but I have been richly blessed as I died to self and decided to empower, lead, and teach people to reach their goals by helping them to maximize their potential.

Name a selfish ambition you've had to deny—and describe how doing so has elevated your attitude.

_____

_____

_____

_____

_____

2. **We must die to our weaknesses.**

In our reasoning and thought processes, our weaknesses will naturally fight against what we have decided to do, waging war against our elevated attitude, causing it to grow _____ and stagnant.

Early in my professional career, there were times I wanted my name to be everywhere. I desired fame and fortune, and I wanted it right away. I didn't want to wait or work for it. I didn't want it even to help people. I wanted it because it was what *I* wanted. My ego and selfish ambition were weaknesses—and they had to die. I had to commit to myself that fame wasn't important. My name didn't need to be everywhere. The only thing that really mattered was serving people.

As I killed those weaknesses, helping others became most important to me. That has allowed me to fulfill the words of the genius theoretical theorist, Albert Einstein. "Try not to become a man of success, but rather try to become a man of value."

LENA'S STORY

Lena's weakness was also her obsession. Her passion to find artifacts from an ancient civilization led her all over the world and left behind a trail of destroyed relationships, including those with her husband and her daughter. At times, her path crossed theirs, and her internal longing to repair and enjoy those relationships would surface. But each time, Lena's inability to recognize her obsession as a weakness drew her away from the only two people who truly cared for her.

Sadly, Lena's tale does not have a happy ending. She lost her life at the end of a yet another archeological expedition. Lena was only 55 years old when she died alone and half a world away from her husband and daughter, both of whom had moved on with their lives without her. Lena selfishly sought success and a sense of purpose apart from her family, and it cost her everything.

Questions for application:

1. Lena's brief story is a very real cautionary tale. As you read it, what specific weakness came to mind that may be negatively impacting your most important personal relationships?

_____

_____

_____

_____

_____

2. Now that you've recognized it, what is the first thing you can do this week to begin addressing it?

_____

_____

_____

_____

_____

3. Envision what it will be like to completely die to that weakness, and describe how doing so would elevate your attitude.

_____

_____

_____

_____

_____

3. We must die to the expectations of society.

Developing an elevated attitude based on a transformed mindset starts by dying to the way society sees success.

There was a time early in my career when I was trying to advance as a young engineer at General Motors. My attitude was simple: get there by any means necessary as long as I didn't do anything illegal. I picked up that mentality at Kettering, where we were taught to be cut-throat in everything we did. Therefore, I wasn't taking into account the feelings and needs of others, and I certainly wasn't a team player. I was in it for myself. That was how society did things.

Then I was challenged by a seasoned engineer about my goals and plans for the future. He told me I was not displaying the right attitude, and he taught me about being a servant leader: a person who can have goals and dreams, but who puts other people and his team first. He helped me to understand that what I wanted to achieve could only be done with the aid of my colleagues. As someone once said, "If you live your life as if everything is about you, you will be left with just that. Just you."

I didn't want that, and I took his advice. As I went to work on a new project, a specific machine for operations, I consulted with everybody on that line. I listened to their ideas and applied them. I asked, "What do you believe will make this work?" "How can I help you achieve that?" I made it about *them*.

When it was time to present the machine to the top brass from headquarters, I declared that we, the team, did it. We accomplished it together.

I got more accolades for that project than anything I had done up to that point. Why? Because I killed society's view of how to be successful and became a servant leader. I chose to _____ others greater than myself.

Name a societal expectation you've had to die to—and describe how doing so has elevated your attitude.

_____

_____

_____

_____

_____

Both an eagle and a chicken are classified as birds. They have wings, and each one can elevate off the surface of the earth. But we can distinguish that a certain bird is an eagle because an eagle flies high on mountain cliffs, will fly into the storm toward the sun, and demands respect as it searches for its prey. A chicken, on the other hand, only flies as high as the barnyard fence. It plucks with its head down toward the ground when looking for food. Its power is trivial compared to the eagle.

I like the chicken, but I am thankful for the wings of an eagle. I don't want to hang out with chickens. I eat chickens. I want to hang out with eagles because they soar high, and I want to fly like one.

That requires confidence—an elevated attitude that we'll explore next.

Attitude Defined **Fill-in-the-Blank Answer Key:**

controls	seeing	others
fulfillment	shaped	weary
journey	agent	esteem
expecting	victor's	
products	future	
greatness	positive	
settle	quiet	

Notes

_____

_____

_____

_____

_____

_____

_____

_____

_____

_____

_____

_____

_____

_____

_____

_____

_____

_____

_____

_____

_____

_____

_____

_____

2

ATTITUDE OF CONFIDENCE

Be strong and courageous in your thoughts and actions.

Frank Lloyd Wright is among the most innovative architects in American history. But his fame wasn't limited to the United States. About 100 years ago, officials in Japan asked Wright to design a hotel for Tokyo that would be capable of surviving an earthquake. When the architect visited Japan to see where the Imperial Hotel was to be built, he was appalled to find only about eight feet of earth on the site. Beneath that was 60 feet of soft mud that slipped and shook like jelly. Every test hole he dug filled up immediately with water.

A lesser man probably would have given up right there. But not Frank Lloyd Wright. Since the hotel was going to rest on fluid ground, Wright decided to build it like a ship. Instead of trying to keep the structure from moving during a quake, he incorporated features that would allow the hotel to ride out the shock without damage. Supports were sunk into the mud, and sections of the foundation were cantilevered from the supports. The rooms were built in sections like a train and hinged together. Water pipes and electric lines, usually the first to shear off in an earthquake, were hung in vertical shafts where they could sway freely if necessary.

Then, on September 1, 1923, Tokyo experienced the greatest earthquake in its history up to that time. There were fires all over the city, and 140,000 people perished. One newspaper wanted to print the story that the Imperial Hotel had been destroyed, as rumor had it. But when a reporter called Frank Lloyd Wright, he said he was confident the hotel would not collapse.

Shortly afterward, Wright got a telegram from Japan. The Imperial Hotel was completely undamaged. Not only that—it had provided a temporary home for hundreds of people.

The Imperial Hotel isn't there anymore. It was torn down in the 1960s to be replaced by a more modern structure.[7] But the legacies of the hotel's strength and Wright's courage to boldly see to its construction remain today.

To have an Attitude of Confidence, we must develop our strength and courage to _____ fast to what we have purposed for our lives. Many people have attitudes of fear and weakness because they do not renew their _____ in the areas of boldness and power. Yet true confidence only comes from elevating our attitude so that our thoughts and actions reflect that confidence.

ANGEL'S STORY

Following successful tours of duty in the Middle East with the United States Army, Angel chose a career in federal law enforcement. His cheerful, almost happy-go-lucky personality, though, served to mask a deep pain from the past—the loss of a fellow soldier under his command—that often worked to accentuate his anxieties and sap his confidence.

After much resistance, Angel started regularly seeing a therapist. Over time, Angel began to strip away those hurtful layers, and as he did, the confrontation of his psychological fears and wounds resulted in a bolstering of his self-assurance and a rejuvenation of his boldness. He became more human, interpersonal, and intuitive in his approach during investigations, and Angel found his sense of duty to job and country infused with more dynamism and strength.

Angel's therapist told him, "You're a healthy man. You can accept what you've done and the pain and sadness and regret that comes with it. You know, not everybody has the strength to deal with that reality." Today, Angel thrives with one legacy in mind: "At the end of the day I want to be someone who's given more than they've taken."

Questions for application:

1. To hold fast to the purpose for our lives, we sometimes have to confront past pain. Briefly describe one hurt that you've had to overcome.

_____

_____

_____

_____

_____

2. How did that confrontation positively impact your confidence?

_____

_____

_____

_____

_____

3. Create a legacy statement similar to Angel's that communicates your current attitude about the future.

_____

_____

_____

_____

_____

Attitude is the father of behavior

No amount of training in leadership skills, courses in management methods, power titles, promotions, or associations can be a substitute for having the right attitude. Attitude is the power of visualized victory, and this mindset is a natural by-product of the _____ of our self-worth, self-esteem, and sense of value or significance.

Incredibly, the average person has as many as 60,000 thoughts a day—and the vast majority of them, 80 percent, are negative. You can offset this trend in your thinking by emotionally esteeming your current goals and your future expectations about them above your present reality. See it, believe it, and act as if it has already happened. Tell yourself, "Yes, I can! I can feel this way. I deserve to feel this way!"

List three of your most common negative thoughts.

1. _____

2. _____

3. _____

For each one, write how you can elevate your attitude in light of your current goals and future expectations.

1. _____

_____

_____

2. _____

_____

_____

3. _____

_____

_____

Self-worth encompasses your attitude as it is impacted by _____ states such as pleasure, triumph, pride, despair, shame, and pain. In their 2007 article on the Rosenberg Self-Esteem Scale Greek Validation on Student Sample, Eliot R. Smith and Diane M. Mackie explained that "self-concept is what we think about the self; self-esteem is the positive or negative evaluations of the self, as in how we feel about it."[8]

Our self-esteem is elevated when we contribute to our society with importance and meaning. When the COVID-19 pandemic first broke out, many people in our community in northern Alabama suffered from a lack of food. They were from all races and all ages, all demographics and all socioeconomic backgrounds, and I had never seen anything like it before.

Ability Plus Inc. in Huntsville, the largest single provider of services for people with special needs in Alabama, and Emmanuel: The Connection Church partnered to give out food boxes one Saturday morning. In all, we gave away a couple thousand boxes of non-perishable food: nuts, rice, cereal, and beans. It was hard, but incredibly rewarding, work. Self-esteem is affirmed when you think and feel good about yourself.

When was the last time you positively contributed to your society or community? Detail your story, ending with how you felt when it was over.

_____

_____

_____

_____

_____

Finally, our sense of value or significance is elevated when we see our _____ and great worth. Violins made by masters like Antonio Stradivari produce an incomparably beautiful sound and sell for millions to investors. But excellent violins are not like works of art, to be hung on a wall or displayed under glass. They'll lose their tone if not played regularly, and they actually increase in value the more they're used. That's why the Stradivari Society exists. It puts those first-rate violins into the hands of great violin virtuosos to ensure the instruments are preserved, cared for, and played. The musicians are even required to give the violin owners two command performances each year.

As you change your mindset about yourself, you will become a virtuoso at whatever you do and in whatever obstacle you face. In fact, your attitude should be the attitude of a king. You must think to rule, not over individuals, but over situations.

Describe a situation in your life right now that you feel you "rule" over, and tell how that attitude affects your confidence.

_____

_____

_____

_____

_____

In essence, our attitude is the _____ of who we think we are, for good or for bad. Attitude dictates our responses to the present and determines the quality of our future. To put it more personally, you are your attitude, and your attitude is you. If you do not control your attitude, it will control you. It will propel you forward or knock you backward. Attitude is always the father of behavior—and when you elevate your mindset, confidence and success will follow.

Attitude also determines your success or failure in any venture in life. More opportunities have been lost, withheld, or forfeited because of a poor attitude than from anything else. More powerful than the pain of the past or the confusion of the present, the right attitude and the confidence it brings can turn darkness to light and make small become big.

EMILY'S STORY

She didn't enter foster care until she was a teenager, but that didn't prevent Emily from experiencing many of the negative outcomes that are possible in the fractured, overwrought system. She was once locked in a car trunk for two days because she accidentally broke a dish, and on another occasion she fled to an elderly neighbor's home only to discover that person had died from natural causes. Since she bounced from home to home during her high school years, Emily was socially awkward and emotionally distant at school, traits that characterized her early adult life.

Despite those setbacks, Emily controlled her attitude. At work, her meticulous attention to detail and relentless dedication to solving problems made her a leader among her peers. At home, her temperance with her own children and the joy she found with her husband made her a beloved mother and wife. She could've been a woman in limbo, unsure of herself or her abilities, but Emily instead chose to have a mindset that wouldn't allow the difficulties of her past to dictate her present and future realities.

Her husband said of Emily, "She doesn't feel the pressure to act or do or say anything that she doesn't want to, and no one can make her. She's made herself. That's what makes her who she is."

Questions for application:

1. Emily mastered her own attitude. In general, are you in control of your attitude, or is it in control of you? In what ways?

_____

_____

_____

_____

_____

2. Think about your current attitude in light of challenges from your past. Is your mindset propeling you forward or knocking you backward? Why?

_____

_____

_____

_____

_____

3. What would you say if someone were to ask you, "What makes you who you are?" Explain.

_____

_____

_____

_____

Attitude directly impacts our decisions, the *quality* of our commitment to those decisions, and how well we *remain* committed to those decisions. Decision-making is a product of our attitude since our attitude helps to form opinions and ideas in daily living. When we are in the process of making a decision, our mindset will determine our choices.

There are six attitudes that produce failure. Let's briefly look at each one.

1. **Arrogance** is defined as an attitude of superiority manifested in an overbearing manner or in presumptuous claims or assumptions. When we have an arrogant attitude, we fail to _____ to constructive criticism and knowledge from others. Many times, this hinders us from making vital decisions that'll cause us to mature personally or help in the strategic growth of an organization.

    1. On a scale of 1-10 (with 10 being the highest), how do you rate your own arrogance?

        _____

    2. Why did you give yourself that score?

        _____

        _____

        _____

        _____

        _____

2. **Judgmentalism** is an attitude that forms opinions about others that are usually harsh and critical in nature. This leads to failure because it negatively affects solid relationships and alienates people. Such relationship bankruptcy leaves us without the _____ we need to grow and move to higher levels in our goals and career.

    1. On a scale of 1-10 (with 10 being the highest), how do you rate your own judgmentalism?

        _____

2. Why did you give yourself that score?

_____

_____

_____

_____

_____

3. **Boastfulness** is an expression of excessive self-pride. This attitude causes us to not fully look at _____ and keeps us from seeing the negative traits or behaviors that we need to improve to avoid failure.

    1. On a scale of 1-10 (with 10 being the highest), how do you rate your own boastfulness?

    _____

    2. Why did you give yourself that score?

    _____

    _____

    _____

    _____

    _____

4. **Comparison** is judging ourselves based on what others are thinking or doing. Events such as a promotion, a divorce, an empty nest, or retirement can cause us to inspect who we are in relation to someone else. This can leave us feeling insecure, anxious, or confused. This is not a healthy mindset and can lead to a slow _____ of our self-esteem.

    1. On a scale of 1-10 (with 10 being the highest), how do you rate your own feelings of comparison to others?

    _____

2. Why did you give yourself that score?

_____

_____

_____

_____

_____

5. **Negative competition** is when we compete with others in such a way that we want to win by any means necessary, even at the expense of others. This attitude shuts down the trust and psychological _____ of a team, and negatively impacts the overall culture of an organization, eating away at teamwork and relationships.

   1. On a scale of 1-10 (with 10 being the highest), how do you rate your own tendency toward negative competition?

   _____

   2. Why did you give yourself that score?

   _____

   _____

   _____

   _____

   _____

6. **Disobedience** is an attitude where we refuse to obey rules or authority. This gives ground to undisciplined actions and leads to _____ failures. Disobedience is dangerous, in that we may feel like we are succeeding when, in reality, destruction is just down the road.

   1. On a scale of 1-10 (with 10 being the highest), how do you rate your own disposition toward disobedience?

   _____

2. Why did you give yourself that score?

_____

_____

_____

_____

_____

Conversely, there are seven attitudes that lead to success.

1. **Humility** is the quality of being humble, and it puts the needs of other people before our own as we think of others ahead of ourselves. This does not draw attention to us, and it can mean acknowledging that we are _____ always right. When we have this attitude, we allow others to achieve their best by not trying to upstage or grandstand anyone else.

    1. On a scale of 1-10 (with 10 being the highest), how do you rate your own humility?

    _____

    2. Why did you give yourself that score?

    _____

    _____

    _____

    _____

    _____

2. **Teachableness** means we are ready to learn and open our hearts to new ideas, pursuits, and dreams. Having this attitude means we are willing to do whatever is necessary to _____ knowledge on a particular subject, allowing us to stay on the top of our profession or excel in our personal lives.

    1. On a scale of 1-10 (with 10 being the highest), how do you rate your own teachableness?

    _____

2. Why did you give yourself that score?

_____

_____

_____

_____

_____

3. **Compassion** is an emotional response to sympathy and creates within us a desire to help others. It encourages us to see a need and not just give lip service to it, but actually take action toward _____ it. It is an attitude that pulls people together to unite around a cause.

   1. On a scale of 1-10 (with 10 being the highest), how do you rate your own compassion?

   _____

   2. Why did you give yourself that score?

   _____

   _____

   _____

   _____

   _____

4. **Generosity** is the willingness to give of our time and our finances to benefit the recipient. Positive things happen when we give of ourselves. Author, salesperson, and motivational speaker, the late Zig Zigler, said, "You can have everything in life you want, if you will just help other people get what they want." An attitude of generosity causes us to be _____, which aids in our maturity and leads to greater success in life.

   1. On a scale of 1-10 (with 10 being the highest), how do you rate your own generosity?

   _____

2. Why did you give yourself that score?

_____

_____

_____

_____

_____

_____

5. **Diligence** is described by author Steven K. Scott in *The Richest Man Who Ever Lived: King Solomon's Secrets to Success, Wealth, and Happiness* as creative persistence, a smart-working effort rightly planned and performed in a timely, efficient, and effective manner to attain a pure and high-quality result. When we display this attitude, success is not an _____ for the future, but an obtainable outcome.

    1. On a scale of 1-10 (with 10 being the highest), how do you rate your own diligence?

    _____

    2. Why did you give yourself that score?

    _____

    _____

    _____

    _____

    _____

6. **Obedience** is compliance with an order, request, or law, or submission to another's authority. It carries with it a social influence connotation that causes others to comply to a certain direction of vision and thought. Obedience leads to _____, enabling us to reach our goals and attain various levels of success.

    1. On a scale of 1-10 (with 10 being the highest), how do you rate your own proclivity toward obedience?

    _____

2. Why did you give yourself that score?

_____

_____

_____

_____

_____

7. **Focus** is the quality of having or producing a clear, visual definition. An attitude of focus lets us clearly see the vision ahead in the midst of many other _____ that try to take our eyes off of what is important. We go where our focus goes. Focus requires us to stay on top of our crafts and keep striving to be better.

MICHAELA'S STORY

Known as a nonconformist and a wild child, it is somewhat stereotypical, then, that Michaela excels as an artist. Degrees in visual arts and computer science provide the credentials for her craft. But that's where the typecast ends and the true motivation of her focus rises to the top. Michaela's free spirted personality is also laced with an inherent empathy toward others that has proven to be an invaluable asset to her family and co-workers. She possesses an acute sense of others' emotions and an ability to interpret those insights to encourage and exhort those around her to become better people.

Michaela attributes this to her own self-awareness. In addition to the mental discipline of meditation, she nurtures physical development and regulation. "We hold on to so much in our bodies," she said. "Yoga helps you let go of things, and it's incredibly grounding." As she maintains her focus, Michaela is empowered to refine her talents as a digital artist and to cultivate the depth of her personal relationships, informed by her unique take on love.

"Some people have this bourgeois notion that in order for love to be real it has to be permanent. Nothing is permanent," she said. "That's just a fact. We move in and out of loving other people, but that doesn't make the love any less real."

Questions for application:

1. I earlier wrote, "We go where our focus goes." Where do you believe your focus is taking you right now in life?

_____

_____

_____

_____

_____

2. How do you feel about your response to Question 1? Be honest.

_____

_____

_____

_____

_____

3. Michaela's distinctive focus on her professional and personal life is nurtured by her self-awareness. What discipline can you begin practicing in your life that will help your focus and elevate your overall attitude?

_____

_____

_____

_____

_____

Developing confidence from self-development

An attitude of success breeds an Attitude of Confidence to discover and live your best life. Confidence is defined as an assurance, trust, or reliance on something or someone—including yourself.

When I first became chief executive officer at Ability Plus, it was failing financially. In addition, internal issues with staffing and leadership had taken their toll, and the people there had no confidence. I needed to trust that I was in that position at that particular time to do something different. Because of that conviction, I wasn't afraid of what would happen down the road, and when there were hard choices, we made them knowing that we would get back to a place higher than where we were before.

That was exactly what happened. I had an opportunity to influence leaders, teammates, and younger professionals by looking at our company's culture. In a year-and-a-half, we dramatically turned around that culture, and the company's bottom line, through teaching and mentorship. I worked with the staff to change their behavior and outlook on what was possible, and that instilled confidence.

When I encourage others, such as my staff at Ability Plus, to do their best, I then challenge them by asking, "Are you sure that is your best?" In the context of where you are right now as a professional, how would you answer my question—and why?

_____

_____

_____

_____

_____

Such confidence does not come automatically. Rather, confidence is an attribute that comes from our diligence reading, studying, and applying positive, self-help techniques such as those found in this workbook. Rem Jackson, founder and CEO of Top Practices, LLC, points out how people usually place a high value on education—up to a point. "However, many people stop actively seeking to learn, develop, and grow different areas of their lives and interests when they graduate and move into the workforce. The most successful businesspeople and medical professionals out there, however, never stop learning, and I don't just mean continuing education or studying for boards. Self-improvement and personal growth are an important, and highly valuable, part of your career and life in general."

He concludes, "Personal growth is a process of both understanding yourself and pushing yourself to reach your highest potential. It means always asking yourself who you are becoming and how you plan to get there."[9]

1. As an ongoing learner, would you characterize yourself as active, neutral, or stagnant?

_____

2. What can you do in the next month to maintain or change that status?

_____

_____

_____

_____

_____

In my corporate presentation entitled "The Champion Mindset," I detail five mentalities that make a leader a champion. One of those is the willingness to learn—and I break that mentality down into three essential steps:

1. **Gather ideas from a variety of sources.** This speaks to the power of *thorough research.* As an engineer, I resonated with Lauren Landry's thoughts regarding the business skills every engineer needs. She wrote, "As technology continues to disrupt industries, the engineers who will advance are those who know how to spot emerging opportunities and validate their ideas. In an increasingly complex global business environment, companies can't keep approaching issues the same way. Engineers play a pivotal role in researching and identifying new business strategies."[10]

    Strong researching abilities are best defined by following the scientific method, which is a tried-and-true systemic approach used to study and understand something by employing the following steps:[11]

    1. Empirical observation: Objective observations using your senses or instruments to gather data.
    2. Formulation of a hypothesis: A testable statement or prediction that proposes an explanation for a specific observation.
    3. Testing and experimentation: Observational studies to test the validity of your hypothesis by gathering data to provide evidence for or against the hypothesis.
    4. Data collection and analysis: Qualitative or quantitative data is then analyzed using statistical methods or other techniques to draw meaningful conclusions.
    5. Reproducibility and verification: Others should be able to replicate the study and obtain similar results to validate the findings. One of the hallmarks of the scientific method is that experiments and observations should be reproducible.
    6. Peer review: Research usually undergoes a peer review process where other subject matter experts evaluate your methodology, results, and conclusions to ensure the quality and credibility of your research.

7. Revision and refinement: The scientific method is an iterative process. New evidence or data may lead to the revision of hypotheses or theories. Therefore, your understanding of something evolves over time.

8. Objectivity and impartiality: Minimizing bias and personal beliefs that could influence your results is mandatory to research excellence.

9. Falsifiability: There should be the possibility of obtaining evidence that contradicts or refutes the proposed explanation. Research findings must be testable and falsifiable.

What do you need to research and thoroughly test to better yourself so that you can grow personally and professionally?

_____

_____

_____

_____

_____

_____

2. **Accurately evaluate a situation based on your knowledge of the situation.** This speaks to the benefit of *informed discernment.* Once you have gathered your ideas, researched them, and thoroughly tested them, you need to apply them. Former president of Cornerstone University, Joseph Stowell, once said that discernment is the skill that "enables us to differentiate. It is the ability to see issues clearly ... We must be prepared to distinguish light from darkness, truth from error, best from better, righteousness from unrighteousness, purity from defilement, and principles from pragmatics."[12]

What do you need to apply from your research to better yourself so that you can grow personally and professionally?

_____

_____

_____

_____

_____

_____

3. **Combine good ideas with the details of the situation to make changes in your behavior personally and organizationally.** This speaks to the outcome of *proactive adaptability*. Expert gardeners know that giving new bedding plants some rough treatment at planting time may be the best thing you can do to help them survive in the garden. If a plant has been growing in its pot so long that the roots are circling the bottom, don't hesitate to jab your finger into the bottom of the soil and pull down to untangle the roots. If you break some of the roots in the process, that's okay. It's far better than allowing the remaining roots to continue to circle when the plant is set into the garden soil.[13]

There's no need to be complacent and comfortable with where you are right now. The healthiest thing you can do is shake up your roots and plant them in new soil. Intentionally adapt and change your present state toward a wiser, more educated future state of self-development.

Using what you have learned, what do you need to **proactively adapt** *in your life to better yourself so that you can grow personally and professionally?*

_____

_____

_____

_____

_____

As you use information to change your situation, you will grow your confidence and elevate your attitude.

T.J.'S STORY

T.J. is an expert gardener—and then some. An entomologist, botanist, and mineralogist, T.J.'s skills make him a preeminent scientist in researching the inner workings of insects, plants, and rocks and soil to determine how each one can be better understood and utilized to benefit humankind while, at the same time, protecting the environment. His proficiency has led colleagues to dub him, "King of the Lab," a moniker T.J. accepts with pride.

The secret to his success is his insatiable desire to learn. He loves using the scientific method, often to extremes. His outlandish experiments included one instance when he implanted a fly beneath his own skin, allowing it to lay its eggs in his neck. His informed discernment based on the findings of his experiments have led to many breakthroughs, and his adaptability has resulted in new research procedures that had never been previously considered, much less tried.

Yet even as his confidence has grown, T.J. has always strived to sustain a realistic attitude about himself and what he can do to preserve his own contentment in life. "The thought of losing so much control over personal happiness is unbearable. That's the burden. Like wings, they have weight, we feel that weight on our backs, but they are a burden that lifts us. Burdens that allow us to fly."

Questions for application:

1. Name a piece of information you learned in the past month that changed you, and describe how it did.

_____

_____

_____

_____

_____

2. How are you now using that information to help grow your confidence and elevate your attitude?

_____

_____

_____

_____

_____

3. Like T.J., do you see your responsibility to preserve your contentment as a beneficial burden? Why or why not?

_____

_____

_____

_____

_____

Signs of a lack of confidence

There are many signs that'll show up if we are not reflecting an Attitude of Confidence. Each one is like a road signal that warns us that we are about to take a wrong turn, and each one will hurt your quest to live your best life.

One sign is *frustration and anxiety*. Both indicate that we are upset about something that is not happening the way we thought it should. Yet we must constantly know and accept that such emotions only extract interest on trouble before it comes due. They constantly drain the energy you need to face daily problems and fulfill your many responsibilities.

1. Describe something that happened in the past week that frustrated you or caused you to be anxious.

   _____

   _____

   _____

   _____

   _____

2. How did you use your mindset to deal with it?

   _____

   _____

   _____

   _____

   _____

3. What would you do differently in the future to elevate your attitude even higher?

   _____

   _____

   _____

   _____

   _____

4. Another sign that we are not reflecting an Attitude of Confidence is *offensiveness*. Many times, offenses come up against us which are designed to knock down our confidence. They may come in the form of a lack of acknowledgment, a correction to a certain negative behavior, or an absence of support. When we allow these offenses to get the best of us, we must be careful not to _____ to their level in retaliation.

One of the rarest of management skills, and one of the most difficult to learn, is the ability to deal with criticism. Constructive criticism shows consideration for other people's feelings and invites their suggestions and cooperation. Criticism that starts out by attacking people and putting them in the position of having to defend themselves often turns small problems into big ones. Usually, the best way to start is with simple, friendly questions or queries that will give people a chance to explain their position without being offended and without getting excited.

Then, after you've listened carefully, suggest the changes you'd like them to make, whatever they are, and see what they think of them. Don't push for an immediate decision if it isn't necessary or if there is still substantial disagreement. Ask them to think it over. Tell them you will, too. Later, if you still believe in the changes you want to make, get together with them again. Explain that you've thought it over carefully and still believe the idea is worth a try. Tell them you feel an obligation to give it a fair chance, and you're counting on them to do the same.[14]

TAMARA'S STORY

A "hard line" woman, Tamara's leadership approach as head of a global market research firm at times put her at odds with junior executives on her staff. She was criticized for her inflexibility, dogged adherence to company policy, and assumed lack of empathy for her employees' professional concerns. At one point, Tamara kept butting heads with one of the firm's top strategists. When word got around that she was threatening to remove that strategist from her position, other staffers told her that if that person was dismissed, they'd leave, too.

Tamara was offended by that show of defiance. She saw it as outright insubordination. That's when her sister, Felicia, intervened, reminding Tamara how often she refused to receive constructive criticism from her or their parents during their upbringing. Felicia encouraged Tamara to step back, carefully evaluate the claims against her leadership, and view the entire situation from a big picture perspective.

It worked. Tamara met first with the top strategist, then with the other workers who were against her possible removal. She asked questions, listened to the responses, and harshly evaluated herself using the same rigid standards she placed on others. Not only did she keep the strategist in the firm, but Tamara also adapted how she thought and behaved as a leader. Over time, Tamara became a trusted and beloved leader, and the firm's results for its clients improved.

Questions for application:

1. When have you been criticized at the workplace? Tell the story.

_____

_____

_____

_____

_____

2. What did you do to deal with it?

_____

_____

_____

_____

_____

3. How did someone else's intervention help you overcome that situation?

_____

_____

_____

_____

_____

The next sign is *jealousy and envy*. There is no need to be jealous or envious of what someone has or something they have done. To envy is to want something which belongs to another person. In contrast, jealousy is the fear that something which we possess will be taken away by another person. Although jealousy can apply to our jobs, our possessions, or our reputations, the word more often refers to anxiety which comes when we are afraid that the affections of a loved one might be lost to a rival.[15] No matter what it is or who you are, there are opportunities for you to be a person of value and success regardless of what others have or want from you. Keep things in perspective.

1. Describe something that happened in the past two weeks that caused you to feel jealous or envious.

   _____

   _____

   _____

   _____

   _____

2. How did you use your mindset to deal with it?

   _____

   _____

   _____

   _____

   _____

3. What would you do differently in the future to elevate your attitude even higher?

   _____

   _____

   _____

   _____

   _____

The final sign that we are not reflecting an Attitude of Confidence is *feeling down on ourselves.* This happens when we do not work out, remove, and destroy the issues at the root of our feelings. We can live in victory and joy as we face our emotions and problems with strength and courage.

Author Leo Buscaglia told this story about his mother and their "misery dinner." It happened the night after his father came home and said it looked as if he would have to go into bankruptcy because his partner had absconded with their firm's funds. His father was discouraged, yet his mother went out and sold some jewelry to buy food for a sumptuous feast. When other members of the family scolded her for it, she told them that "the time for joy is now, when we need it most, not next week." Her act rallied his father and their entire family.[16]

1. Describe something that happened in the past month that caused you to feel down on yourself.

   _____

   _____

   _____

   _____

   _____

2. How did you use your mindset to deal with it?

   _____

   _____

   _____

   _____

   _____

3. What would you do differently in the future to elevate your attitude even higher?

   _____

   _____

   _____

   _____

   _____

In his autobiography, *Taken on Trust*, Terry Waite recounted his horrendous experience as a hostage in Beirut prisons for 1,763 days, almost four years of which were spent in solitary confinement. His first cell, underground, measured seven feet by 10 feet. The height varied between six and seven feet. Although living in such cramped quarters, Waite made himself walk. Some days he estimated he walked seven miles. Day and night were indistinguishable. He was led to the bathroom once each day.

Early in his detainment, Waite vowed that his captors would not capture his confidence. "Whatever is done to my body," he determined, "I will fight to the end to keep my inner freedom." He discovered that prayer and fasting increased his emotional strength. From memory, he recited the communion service regarded in the *Book of Common Prayer*.

A man who had once served as envoy for the Archbishop of Canterbury and had personally negotiated hostage releases had himself become the hostage—yet he accepted his situation and recited the mantra, "No regrets, no sentimentality, no self-pity."[17]

Terry Waite not only retained an Attitude of Confidence, he exercised incredible control of his emotions. Such emotional intelligence is vital to elevating your attitude, as you'll discover in the next chapter.

Attitude of Confidence **Fill-in-the-Blank Answer Key:**

hold	support	solving
minds	ourselves	sacrificial
integration	decline	option
emotional	safety	discipline
uniqueness	systemic	distractions
manifestation	not	stoop
listen	gain	

Notes

_____

_____

_____

_____

_____

_____

_____

_____

_____

_____

_____

_____

_____

_____

_____

_____

_____

_____

_____

_____

_____

_____

_____

3

ATTITUDE OF EMOTIONAL INTELLIGENCE

*Give thought and self-reflection
to the emotional situations you encounter.*

Many people get upset when pressures at work, frustrations at home, and other taxing life issues come upon them. When we don't have proper control over these situations, our attitude will reflect this through negative behavior.

According to Travis Bradberry, author of *Emotional Intelligence 2.0*, emotional intelligence is our ability to recognize and understand emotions in ourselves and others, and to use this awareness to manage our behavior and relationships. Daniel Goleman, regarded as the father of emotional intelligence (also known as emotional quotient or EQ), says EQ is managing feelings so that they are expressed appropriately and effectively, enabling people to work together smoothly toward their common goals. EQ expert Steve Hein defines emotional intelligence as the combination of innate emotional sensitivity with learned emotional management skills, which together lead to long-term happiness and survival.

When we first become _____ of our own emotions and those of others, we can start to _____ our attitude in such a way as to produce positive change and results.

Therefore, to have self-control over our emotions, and the emotional reactions of others toward us, is an Attitude of Emotional Intelligence.

What is your worst emotional trigger? Circle one.

Technology glitches

Financial difficulties

Relationship issues

Medical problems

Why is your chosen trigger a problem for you?

_____

_____

_____

_____

_____

Our attitude is a product of our behavior and is based on our self-esteem, self-image, and self-efficacy (how well we respond to potential situations). We must monitor our Attitude of Emotional Intelligence daily to produce the positive mindset and behavior needed to get the desired results. It is very important that we continually work on managing what we feel and how our feelings affect others.

This is not something that just happens. We need to grow intentionally by placing our personal development on the _____. We must give much thought and self-reflection to the emotional situations that we encounter every day. We can control our thoughts, and the attitudes that stem from them, when we understand them. I believe everyone wants to have the right attitude in times of peril, stress, and even triumph, but we often haven't developed the mindset to produce that attitude.

Emotional intelligence is commonly defined by five skills:

1. **Self-awareness** is the ability to recognize our own emotions and how they affect our thoughts and behavior. It also helps us to _____ our strengths and weaknesses, and to have self-confidence.

    1. On a scale of 1-10 (with 10 being the highest), how do you rate your own self-awareness?

    _____

    2. Why did you give yourself that score?

    _____

    _____

    _____

    _____

2. **Self-management** is the ability to understand changing situations and manage our feelings and behaviors in a healthy way. This produces a greater _____ of commitment and enables us to take on new and challenging things.

   1. On a scale of 1-10 (with 10 being the highest), how do you rate your own self-management?

      _____

   2. Why did you give yourself that score?

      _____

      _____

      _____

      _____

      _____

3. **Social awareness** is having empathy. This is the capacity to put ourselves in other people's shoes so we can feel their pain. We can do this by learning to understand their behavioral patterns, the differences in their personality types and temperaments, and being able to _____ through those differences.

   1. On a scale of 1-10 (with 10 being the highest), how do you rate your own social awareness?

      _____

   2. Why did you give yourself that score?

      _____

      _____

      _____

      _____

      _____

4. **Relationship management** is the ability to influence other people to behave better and manage their own feelings. We do this by developing and maintaining good relationships, communicating clearly, inspiring others to _____ well in a team environment, and mediating conflict.

    1. On a scale of 1-10 (with 10 being the highest), how do you rate your own relationship management?

       _____

    2. Why did you give yourself that score?

       _____

       _____

       _____

       _____

       _____

5. **Self-motivation** is a personal drive to improve and achieve, a commitment to goals and vision, and a desire to _____ on opportunities with optimism and resilience.

    1. On a scale of 1-10 (with 10 being the highest), how do you rate your own self-motivation?

       _____

    2. Why did you give yourself that score?

       _____

       _____

       _____

       _____

       _____

As we grow in these EQ skills, we will improve our mindset to produce an Attitude of Emotional Intelligence. Let's take a closer, personal look at each one of these skills from that perspective.

Skill 1: Self-awareness

You must know yourself. That knowledge arms you to manage yourself effectively. If you are a stranger to your emotions, fears, or even your purpose, you will live a strange life, one not meant for you, and you will be helpless to the waves of emotions that will drive your actions and decisions wherever they please. This will result in you _____ on other people to define you, and you will be ruled by their opinions of you.

Yet I believe the power to define is the power to determine destiny. As a CEO, I constantly do self-reflections to better understand my emotions in critical situations. I don't act without first running my reactions through a series of filters. I ask myself questions such as, "Is this beneficial to me or the process?" "What does it take to get it done?" "Is this the proper time?" The answers to these questions slow me down just enough to process my emotions and think through the decision I am about to make. They ensure that I am not permitting my opinions to sway me or allowing a vibe that has no legitimacy to persuade me. I am able to get past *me* and get to the issue at hand.

MICHAEL'S STORY

Ever since he came into his own as a teenager, Michael has had a strong sense of who he is and why he thinks and acts the way he does. Driven by his own innate sense of justice, Michael empathizes with those who have been wrongly victimized and seeks to punish those who have harmed them. Though some describe his tactics as unorthodox or over the top, Michael's work as a public defender is unparalleled.

This burgeoning self-awareness has come with its challenges. Michael has an incessant need to control himself and others, guided by a code of conduct handed down to him from his father that Michael views as non-negotiable. In addition, he suffers from a sense of superiority where he believes he possesses higher moral values than those he opposes and, sometimes, the people he represents. While Michael has cordial relationships with his co-workers, he struggles with deeper or romantic interpersonal connections, often feeling awkward and out of his comfort zone.

Michael is working on his EQ to recognize and understand emotions in himself and others while managing his feelings so that they are expressed appropriately and effectively. He is doing this by spending more time with his sister, Deb, and developing his rapport with his girlfriend, Darla. Regarding his continuing journey toward greater self-awareness, Michael told Deb, "I dream I'm floating on the surface of my own life. Watching it all unfold. Observing it. The outsider looking in."

Questions for application:

1. How well do you believe you know yourself? Explain.

_____

_____

_____

_____

_____

2. What is the biggest challenge you've run into as you've tried to become more self-aware?

_____

_____

_____

_____

_____

3. Do you feel like Michael, an outsider looking in on yourself, or are you more intimate with your own self-awareness at this stage of your life? Why?

_____

_____

_____

_____

_____

Skill 2: Self-management

Self-management is the ability to train your mind to strengthen and increase in capacity so that it is empowered to accept your feelings and maximize its energy to exhibit the right behavior, attitude, actions, and words. Your mind is like a knife. If you sharpen it, it cuts faster. If you don't, it becomes dull and inefficient.

Your mind is one of the greatest gifts you possess to help you live a successful life. But the imperfections associated with living dump a lot of junk into your mind. So, to get the best out of your mind, that junk has to be _____ out so your mind can be refurbished. A refurbished mind will help you maintain the right perception, and that's vital since you respond to issues based on what you perceive about them. Through self-management, your mind is refurbished to allow its full potential to be reaped. Mind management takes care of personal and emotional management, and well managed emotions enable you to act, talk, and respond to issues in the right way, place, and time to the right people, as opposed to reacting to them.

I'm quite intentional about managing my feelings and desires. There have been certain things that I felt like I needed right away, but I used the self-management strategy of delayed gratification to put them off for a more appropriate time. Delayed gratification is beneficial because it creates the time to build money, talent, or resources in order to obtain something. Then, when the opportune moment arrives, you'll have everything you need to be as productive and successful as possible.

JENNIFER'S STORY

She just wanted to be noticed for her abilities. But in a workplace dominated by men and an archaic "good 'ol boy" code, it was hard for Jennifer to attain the recognition she rightfully deserved. This frustrated her for a long time, and the fact that she could easily be impulsive and even crass didn't help her attitude.

Then Jennifer was encouraged by her nephew, Harrison, to train her mind to be more disciplined and patient in her circumstances. Applying his advice, Jennifer doubled down on her work ethic while beginning to fill her thoughts with the positive things she already had in her life so that she'd be more equipped to wait for her professional redemption. She also recognized that while she was not at all shy and could be quite headstrong, beneath that tough persona was a sensitive and caring individual that would empower her perseverance and restraint, even if she didn't readily express it. In the end, her skill set was perceived and recognized by leadership, and Jennifer was promoted not once, but twice, over the following four years.

Jennifer continues working on her EQ to recognize and understand emotions in herself and others while managing her feelings so that they are expressed appropriately and effectively by being more present. "Practice being in the moment when you are running, whether you are on your own or in the race," she said. "One of the things I've started doing lately is tracking my dreams. There's a lot of information there, and you can really bring those emotions to the situations that may feel mundane or familiar."

Questions for application:

1. How well do you believe you manage yourself? Explain.

    _____

    _____

    _____

    _____

    _____

2. What is the biggest challenge you've faced as you've tried to become better at self-management?

    _____

    _____

    _____

    _____

3. Would you consider tracking your dreams, like Jennifer is doing, as a self-management tool? Why or why not?

    _____

    _____

    _____

    _____

    _____

Skill 3: Social awareness

Social awareness is a social skill that enables you to maintain harmony in your world through an existing inner peace. When you are able to understand other people's feelings and relate better to them, social awareness usually leads to positive action.

Result-oriented social awareness must be _____. You will need to study peoples' personality types to be able to understand their emotions. Through personality types, you will understand why others act, react, or talk a certain way. All three are the overflow of their emotional state. So, social awareness understands this and devises a means for you to manage them.

I have learned how to put myself in other people's shoes and try to understand their point of view. Once, one of our Ability Plus house managers came to me. He oversaw staff and programs for several of the homes we serve. He told me, "We need more funding because our responsibility is to fulfill what the budget demands." So, I shadowed him for a few days to assess his concern and find out what his days were like. In doing so, I discovered that we actually didn't need to put more resources into the homes. Instead, we pulled back on some things so that the house manager could improve his planning and overall leadership. It also made me more empathetic to the concerns he was dealing with, which he appreciated.

DAVID'S STORY

David made a promise to his beloved father when his dad was on his deathbed, pledging to be totally honest with others in his personal and professional life. However, that dedication to forthrightness got David in trouble. First, he exposed a popular co-worker's wrongdoing to human resources, resulting in a backlash from many of his peers at the real estate office. Second, he confessed having an affair to his wife, resulting in a separation that ultimately led to the end of their marriage. As he told a friend one night at a restaurant bar after the divorce was finalized, "I destroyed my marriage. I lost my little girl. I'm a divorced broker halfway down the road to a full-blown cliché, a divorced, alcoholic broker." David was in despair.

That same friend, however, shared something revelatory that night: he told David about his faith in God. His friend's previously unshared tale about how he had found, and was still discovering, inner peace through his religious faith pierced David's heart and left him wanting to know more. He stopped drinking, and over the next several weeks, David accompanied his friend to church and made a decision to follow God. It brought David a social awareness that not only helped him recover from his own errors, but it affirmed his commitment to honesty and integrity. He left his toxic work environment, completely switched gears, and began working in the kitchen at the very restaurant where he'd taken his final drink with his friend. He excelled and advanced. Within five years, David owned the restaurant.

David is working on his EQ to recognize and understand emotions in himself and others while managing his feelings so that they are expressed appropriately and effectively. He is doing this by pursuing the tenets of his faith and daily applying them to his thoughts, decisions, and actions. To this day, he refers to his friend as his "earthly angel."

Questions for application:

1. How well do you believe you maintain harmony in your world through an existing inner peace? Explain.

   _____

   _____

   _____

   _____

   _____

2. What is the biggest challenge you've faced as you've tried to become more socially aware through inner peace?

   _____

   _____

   _____

   _____

   _____

3. What does David's redemption story tell you about your own past?

   _____

   _____

   _____

   _____

   _____

Skill 4: Relationship management

Relationship management is the ability to influence other people to behave better and manage their own feelings. Having good social skills and interpersonal relationships is a major facet of managing other people. You will always have to _____ with other people. Learning this skill is vital in order to relate well with others in the workplace, at home, or in any group.

People have different temperaments, likes, and dislikes, and they bring different kinds of energy and understanding to situations. These differences will play out in the way they act, respond, or talk—so if you can manage those differences, you can maintain peace and maximize the benefits of those relationships.

I often teach others about their value and worth both to themselves and to their organizations. One time, I brought all of our mid-level managers together to participate in teamwork exercises designed to enhance our concern for one another and help overall production. These exercises focused on what they would do if they were in their peer's position in the company. They asked questions like, "What decisions would you make?" "How would you act?" We had role play sessions to help everyone appreciate what each person was doing and how each one brought value to the company. It built better relationships among the management team.

JAMES' STORY

As a worker, his career in law enforcement required James to manage all manner of relationships—but his most important relationship, the one that needed his utmost attention by far, was the one with his adopted son, Morgan. Exposed to unspeakable trauma before coming into his family as a small child, James had to lovingly, patiently, and consistently help Morgan deal with the darkness of his past, especially as the boy navigated the often icy and choppy waters of adolescence.

To aid himself, James studied different personality and temperament models and read books on child therapy so that he could better understand what Morgan was going through and advise him accordingly. If Morgan had a question, James was there. Whenever Morgan lashed out with cutting, angry sarcasm or got into altercations at school, James intervened and talked Morgan through his conflicting emotions. Most of all, he made sure Morgan knew he was accepted and cared for, encouraging his son not to define himself solely by what had occurred in his life as a boy, but by who he was in the present and could become in the future. "It's okay," James often told his son. "You can't help what happened to you. But you can make the best of it. Remember this forever, you are my son. You are not alone, and you are loved.""

James is working on his EQ to recognize and understand emotions in himself and others while managing his feelings so that they are expressed appropriately and effectively. He is doing this by regularly receiving counseling himself to energize his efforts as a father and deal with his own feelings as he does.

Questions for application:

1. In general, are you more at ease or more uncomfortable dealing with other people? Explain your answer.

_____

_____

_____

_____

_____

2. What is the biggest challenge you've faced as you've tried to manage your family relationships? Why?

_____

_____

_____

_____

_____

3. What are you doing to help yourself as you manage all of the relationships in your life? Can you do more?

_____

_____

_____

_____

_____

Skill 5: Self-motivation

Self-motivation is the ability to stir yourself to do what needs to be done without influence from other people. Another word for self-motivation is self-encouragement. Self-motivated people are enthusiastic. They have the ability to complete a task even in the face of barriers.

A crucial part of self-motivation is _____ making. This can be daunting, and it can pull strongly on your emotions. Making hard decisions is not always easy, and it can be damaging if not properly handled. Every decision has consequences, and your decisions today will determine your quality of life tomorrow. Your decisions sculpt your destiny.

One of the things I do to motivate myself is to tell myself there are *no* bad days. I've chosen to never give in to disappointment and be sorry for an entire day. So, I gave each day a special name that I call, sign, and profess. For example, I call Sunday "Super Sunday." I sign it that day by using "Super Sunday" in my electronic messages. I profess it by saying "It's a Super Sunday" aloud throughout the day. I also came up with Marvelous Monday, Terrific Tuesday, Wonderful Wednesday, Triumphant Thursday, Fantastic Friday, and Successful Saturday!

These started out as nothing more than titles, but I have since developed attributes, characteristics, and principles to go with each one, creating material to teach from these concepts. As a result, my self-motivation technique has become a powerful way to motivate others. One of my colleagues and a dear friend, Dr. Claudette Owens, attended a professional luncheon in 2022 where I was the keynote speaker. As told in her extraordinary book, *Recapturing Our Lost Identity: Overcoming the power brokers of greed and hate with the superpowers of love*, something amazing happened.

"As soon as I sat down," she wrote, "I could sense that something was going on inside the young lady to my right. Being able to feel what other people are feeling is nothing new to me. As I sat there next to this woman, that feeling became stronger and heavier … Doc Rock was talking about not allowing yourself to have a bad day, but giving yourself a couple of moments, or a couple of hours at the most, to deal with negative or trying circumstances. He exhorted us that we should not allow those situations to control our entire day. Yet I could tell that the young lady next to me was troubled about something to the point that she was on the verge of giving up."

Claudette continued, "As Doc Rock instructed us to repeat the phrase, 'No bad days,' she looked at me and said, 'I'm trying.' Before I realized what I was doing, I reached for her hand, pulled her close to me, and spoke quietly into her ear. 'Life comes with uncertain blows. Some will even knock you down. That's okay. You have to get up, dust yourself off, and keep moving. The key to reaching our goals in life is to keep going in the right direction. Some days, you may move at a snail's pace; others, you may move in sheer faith; and others still, you may move in pain. But the key is to keep moving. Moving is the only way you arrive at your destination. When you stop, you either enter a long layover or end up staying in a location you were never destined to be in. So, keep moving.' The smile that came to her face was priceless."

Claudette possessed the emotional intelligence to stir that woman to be self-motivated and find the inner strength to proceed.

JULIE'S STORY

The blows that came into Julie's life, unfortunately, were literal. An abusive marriage not only scarred Julie's physical body, but it blurred her psyche. After escaping her dangerous husband and securing a divorce, Julie carried on more than capably as a single mother, but she was awkward around other people and timid when handling minor confrontations with neighbors. When she was finally able to welcome a kind and caring man into her life, she avoided having a sexual relationship with him because of the lingering effects of her past trauma.

Thanks to the patience and care she received from her boyfriend, as well as the enduring love she gained from her children, Julie was able to heal. With each new month, Julie worked on her own to make decisions that had more positive outcomes, and she practiced self-encouragement by developing a daily routine of mindfulness and meditation. One of her daily mantras stated, "The past can be remembered, and it can be learned from. But the past no longer exists. It cannot be changed. It cannot be reset. It cannot be undone. All that I have is the present and the potential of the future, and that is more than enough for me."

Julie continues to work on her EQ to recognize and understand emotions in herself and others while managing her feelings so that they are expressed appropriately and effectively by keeping a forward-thinking perspective. "At the end of the day, when you're on your death bed and that's it, I think it's the relationships you've had and the people that you've touched and the people that have touched you that matter."

Questions for application:

1. What have you overcome to be equipped to stir yourself to do what needs to be done without influence from other people? Tell the story.

_____

_____

_____

_____

_____

2. When you first read my statement, "Your decisions sculpt your destiny," what was the first thing that came to mind? Be honest.

_____

_____

_____

_____

_____

3. What can you begin doing this week to elevate your attitude after considering your response to Question #2?

_____

_____

_____

_____

_____

As I stated earlier, an Attitude of Emotional Intelligence is not something that just happens. It has to be practiced daily and consistently.

BetterMe writer Clare Kamau's article, "Examples Of Emotional Intelligence To Practice In Daily Life," presented a scenario where someone in your life did something that you had already asked them not to do. She wrote that an emotionally intelligent person would:

- Recognize you are feeling angry that the other person disregarded your words and feelings.

- Realize that your anger makes you want to shout at or avoid the person, but that doesn't solve the situation. You may choose to walk away for the time being and perhaps journal or meditate to allow yourself to calm down.

- Once you've calmed down, you can approach the offending person, talk to them in private, and discuss the situation, expressing how the crossing of set boundaries made you feel. You can try to understand why the person did it regardless of your opinion. You can also assert that it will not be allowed to happen again.

- Actively listen to the other person's explanation with an open heart and mind and try to understand the person's feelings and find common ground.[18]

1. In her article, Clare detailed a systematic approach to dealing with anger. Of those four steps, which one do you feel you are weakest at...and why?

   _____

   _____

   _____

   _____

   _____

2. Of those four steps, which one do you feel you are strongest at...and why?

   _____

   _____

   _____

   _____

   _____

Having and using emotional intelligence is all about elevating your attitude and applying your _____ to recognize and understand emotions in yourself and others in each individual situation. Juanita Fourie, a creative writer in South Africa, posted on Quora two more practical stories of emotional intelligence in everyday life. She shared the following:

1. It is Saturday afternoon and, after having worked six consecutive days of 14 hours each, Michelle finally gets to leave the office.

While stuck in traffic on her way home, the normally calm Michelle shouts a string of unsavory words at a group of cyclists snaking irresponsibly through the cars. On top of her boiling rage, she is suddenly reminded of her more-than-20-years-ago student days and the many lovely afternoons of cycling she and her first serious boyfriend enjoyed. Suddenly, she is overwhelmed by an intense feeling of nostalgia, which soon turns into great sadness that sees her breaking down into uncontrollable tears.

"Don't worry, Michelle," she tells herself while taking a deep breath. "You are just tired and overemotional."

Michelle understands her emotions and knows that they are coming from a place of lethargy following an unusually demanding workweek. She knows that a long, hot bath and a good night's rest will see her back to her old self in no time.

a. What do you like best about Michelle's response?

_____

_____

_____

_____

_____

b. What do you believe she could have done differently and still had a positive outcome?

_____

_____

_____

_____

_____

2. Sam and his girlfriend just had a terrible fight. Knowing that getting out of the apartment would do him good, Sam decides to take a walk to the nearby park.

On his way there, he sees his nosy neighbor, Jim, along with Jim's irritating little mutt, walking toward him. Sam is most definitely not in the best of moods right now, and the last thing he needs is Jim's endless small talk and that ill-mannered dog of his trying to pee on Sam's new Puma trainers.

As Jim and his fur ball approach, Sam takes a deep breath, calms himself, and greets his neighbor with a pleasant, "Hello, Jim!"

Sam thinks rationally about his anger and knows that it is not Jim's fault he is feeling this way. He knows that acting out toward his innocent neighbor would therefore be nothing short of unfair.[19]

a. What do you like best about Jim's response?

_____

_____

_____

_____

_____

b. What do you believe he could have done differently and still had a positive outcome?

_____

_____

_____

_____

_____

As we develop new levels of mental and emotional self-management through an Attitude of Emotional Intelligence, we become more productive, more creative, and more responsive to the particular _____ of others.

For example, a positive organizational climate is created through leaders and team members who are internally aware of their emotions and those of others, and who are able to understand what is happening inside the organization with its business potential and people. Unless they create an environment that fosters mental and emotional balance by providing the information and motivation needed to help their people develop new self-management skills, organizations cannot expect to see long-term sustainable success in today's social and business world.

Of course, a reality that both individuals and companies deal with on an ongoing basis is money management. Our attitude toward money should be one of mission and purpose. Money is not just to spend, but to be a tool for life improvement—as we'll see next.

Attitude of Emotional Intelligence **Fill-in-the-Blank Answer Key:**

aware	navigate	observant
manage	work	relate
forefront	act	decision
know	depending	ability
level	cleared	needs

4

ATTITUDE OF MONEY

Money is a resource, not the source of your identity.

The O'Jays sang about it back in the day: *Money, money, money, money—money!* They lamented of the drawbacks and hailed the benefits of the almighty dollar on society, and rightly concluded that "money can drive some people out of their minds!"

Everyone needs it, some want lots of it, and many love it, but far fewer people have a proper attitude about it. I totally believe that we can have millions, even billions, of dollars if we work hard for it—and the more money we have, the more we can do to help make a _____ in this world.

I believe wealth and prosperity are blessings, but many people don't see or use their wealth that way because of their _____ attitude toward money. We must learn to look at money—not as the source of who we are, but as a resource to get things done and make a positive difference.

What is money for?

Many people want to be rich, have plenty, and never have to rely on anything else. With all of their financial and material needs fulfilled, they'll never be in need, and therefore will never have to turn to anyone but themselves as their provider.

Yet we must understand that even the millionaire must continue to go higher with his life's aspirations in order to experience true life fulfillment. Money exists so that we may use it _____, not selfishly—and we are enabled to use money properly only because we have elevated our attitude about its use, misuse, and purpose.

MATTHEW'S STORY

He's generally viewed by others as being a genius, and for good reason. Matthew's intensely analytical thinking is fed by his voracious affinity for reading and scrutinizing information at an incredible 15,000 words per minute. He also possesses an eidetic memory that allows him to remember a huge amount of data with exceptional detail. Such skills have proven to be ideally suited for Matthew's career choice as a theoretical physicist during which he has earned doctorates in many disciplines including mathematics and engineering.

But Matthew, while never officially diagnosed, regularly deals with symptoms of mental illness. He has been clinically identified with conditions such as autism, Asperger's Syndrome, and even mild schizophrenia, yet none hinder Matthew in his work. If anything, he'd argue they are more helpful than harmful. Atill, he monitors them and his psychological health with the ongoing aid of a therapist.

Matthew's career has left him well compensated. Therefore, he has chosen to use a significant percentage of his earnings to support organizations that help mentally challenged individuals. Whether it be the National Alliance on Mental Health or the Anxiety and Depression Association of America, Matthew is generous. His altruism is informed by his unique perspective. "Sometimes," he said, "the only difference between insanity and genius is success."

Questions for application:

1. Perhaps you don't see yourself as being a genius, but how would you describe your more unique gifts or abilities? List them here.

_____

_____

_____

_____

_____

2. How have you utilized those talents to build financial prosperity?

_____

_____

_____

_____

_____

3. Name one organization you support financially and cite why you do. If you don't give to a non-profit entity, name a cause you would support if you could and why you would do so.

_____

_____

_____

_____

_____

Because of the systematic cycle we face each day, particularly in the workplace, it can be easy as employees or leaders to subconsciously begin placing our confidence in money, but we must avoid this tendency. Dr. I.V. Hilliard declared five things that should alert us that we have put too much trust in money.

1. **When my worth and esteem is determined by what I possess.** There was a young, up-and-coming man who believed that his importance came from the things he possessed. In fact, the more he bought, the better he felt about himself. He had a mentor who saw his potential and took the time to talk to him about developing a mindset of self-worth that was centered around principles of hard work and dedication. That attitude of self-esteem redefined how he thought about himself and brought new purpose to his life.

   a. How much do you believe your importance comes from the things you possess? Be honest in your self-evaluation.

   _____

   _____

   _____

   _____

   _____

b. What can you begin doing to develop your mindset of self-worth based on hard work and dedication?

_____

_____

_____

_____

_____

2. **When a change in my financial state causes a change in how I treat others.** After securing a promotion, a company leader began treating his fellow team members disrespectfully. He looked down on everyone and didn't even acknowledge some of them. He made decisions without asking others on his team how they felt about it because he believed he was the big man in town.

Not until a true friend challenged his attitude of disrespect and taught him about servant leadership (see next chapter) did he realize that what he was doing was wrong. The leader was a smart guy who had great skills, but people follow others not because of their wits, charisma, or status, but because they trust and believe in that person. He developed an attitude where he put others first, and everything changed—including his misplaced confidence in money to define who he was and how he behaved.

a. List three reasons why you follow others.

1. _____

2. _____

3. _____

b. Now, why do you think people follow you—and what do you want to change, if anything, about that?

_____

_____

_____

_____

_____

3. **When I begin to rationalize why I should not give what I should.** There was a young lady who had been giving regularly to charitable organizations from her monthly pay. However, after a large sum of money was awarded to her, she decided that she had given enough and wanted to keep all of it for herself. She was challenged by her father, one of my colleagues, who reminded her that she'd been doing some good things and pointed her to principles that encouraged rather than corrected her. She chose to reinstate her practice of giving.

    What would you have done in the same situation? Why?

    _____

    _____

    _____

    _____

    _____

4. **When I choose to violate proper principles of conduct to gain money.** An organization that was doing well in its particular industry had an opportunity to gain more market share— but that chance was compromised when an annual audit of its operations and finances revealed some problems. The operations audit looked at what the organization did to ensure that it was following guidelines and principles for that industry, while the financial audit was designed to make sure the company's money was being allocated properly and that everything was on the straight and narrow taxwise. The organization's money was being so severely and fraudulently mismanaged that the CEO was fired, and new leadership was brought in to reinstate principles of responsibility and accountability.

    a. What situation or set of circumstances would motivate you to actually commit financial fraud? Be honest in your self-evaluation.

    _____

    _____

    _____

    _____

    _____

b. What do you think is the root emotion behind that decision—and why?

_____

_____

_____

_____

_____

5. **When my financial state is valued above my integrity.** When someone esteems what's in their pocketbook over their values, then their attitude about money is in error. Wanting to use money as a power source—to buy friendships or to maneuver and deceive people—instead of as a resource, reveals greed and self-centeredness.

A.J.'S STORY

Her role as the media spokesperson for a giant pharmaceutical firm belied her shy, sheltered upbringing in a small Pennsylvania town, but A.J.'s motivation to be the public face and communications liaison for the corporation came from a dark, negative place in her childhood. A.J. was haunted by the memory of her sister's suicide and the trauma it caused her and her family. That pain galvanized and compelled her to gradually become self-absorbed and, when she became a young career woman, self-indulgent. She craved money and influence.

Unfortunately, A.J.'s self-obsession led to her downfall when a decision to leak proprietary information about the firm to a major network reporter, and the rich buyout she received from that network, was exposed. Her choice to maneuver around and deceive her employer for financial gain and the perceived reputation as an insider source that she gained as a result, cost her everything.

Since her incarceration, A.J. has had ample time to examine the folly of her ways, as well as take a hard look at her integrity. "There are things we don't want to happen but have to accept. There are things we don't want to know but have to learn. And there are people we can't live without but have to let go," she told her friend, Emily, during a visitation at the prison. "My inability to let go of my sister destroyed any integrity I had as a kid. Now I have to find it once again."

Questions for application:

1. How would you define your own sense of integrity?

   _____

   _____

   _____

   _____

   _____

2. Looking at that definition, has your self-efficacy (belief in your own integrity) ever been challenged by what's in your pocketbook? Explain how.

   _____

   _____

   _____

   _____

   _____

3. What personal core value can you identify that will prevent you from ever sacrificing your integrity for self-centeredness or greed? Write it here.

   _____

   _____

   _____

   _____

The proper philosophy about money

You'll recall that philosophy is "loving the way we think," and we should love the way we _____ money. That includes understanding its potential pitfalls.

You've undoubtedly heard of "King Solomon's Mines." The subject of both popular literature and motion pictures, the monarch at the center of those stories is actually based on a real person from antiquity: the legendary biblical king renowned both for his wealth and his wisdom. A passage attributed to him in the Old Testament book of Ecclesiastes is entitled "The Foolishness of Riches," and it communicates one of Solomon's core philosophical conclusions about money and wealth.

"Whoever loves money never has enough; whoever loves wealth is never satisfied with their income. This too is meaningless. As goods increase, so do those who consume them. And what benefit are they to the owners except to feast their eyes on them? The sleep of a laborer is sweet, whether they eat little or much, but as for the rich, their abundance permits them no sleep."[20] Solomon believed monetary wealth could bring anxiety, so he finished that chapter by concluding that a person should find fulfillment in whatever lot he finds himself.

The foolishness of riches is quite real. Foolishness is defined as a lack of good judgement—and many people lack _____ about the purpose of money. When we don't know the purpose of something, abuse is inevitable. We may spend all we gain for personal pleasure rather than engaging in delayed gratification, which is an essential practice to being a good steward that brings stability and prosperity in the long run.

JOE'S STORY

Over dinner, Joe confided to his lifelong friend, Jason, "My wife always said I had a flair for the dramatic."

"Really?" Jason replied. "Which one?"

Joe quipped, "All of them."

He wasn't lying. Married and divorced three times, Joe's track record with romantic relationships spoke for itself. Yet it was what happened with his final wife that came with a double whammy of consequences. When they received a large tax refund, instead of saving some, or most, of that money to pay off their bills and investing a portion of it, he spent every penny of it on household improvements. That choice wasn't bad in and of itself, but if he had better discerned how to use the refund, Joe and his wife could've reduced their massively accumulated debt while making some minor improvements on their home. By misusing the refund, Joe had a nicer house but he also placed them in dire financial jeopardy. By doing so without his wife's agreement, he broke the last straw of mistrust that ended their marriage.

Joe couldn't afford to pay for that dinner with Jason because he had just declared bankruptcy. He had been foolish with his money—and so much more. It took consistent, concerted, and long-term help from Jason to help Joe get back on his feet.

Questions for application:

1. Describe how you would help Joe if you were in Jason's place.

    _____

    _____

    _____

    _____

    _____

2. Do you believe it is true that "whoever loves money never has enough; whoever loves wealth is never satisfied with their income?" Why or why not?

    _____

    _____

    _____

    _____

    _____

3. What do you think is the primary purpose of money? Explain your answer.

    _____

    _____

    _____

    _____

    _____

While nice houses, automobiles, jewelry, or fancy clothing have their place for enjoyment in our lives, feeding the hungry, clothing the naked, and providing shelter for those who have no place to sleep is of far more _____ to others. So is providing education for those less fortunate than ourselves, giving them an opportunity to be in an environment geared for success.

Money is needed to achieve all of these needs—and each one allows you to use it as a resource to make your world a better place. There is a great organization I have worked with over the years in Honduras that builds schools, feeds the poor, and trains individuals to make a productive living. I made several trips to Honduras with this organization, doing everything from field work to leadership training. In addition, a company in our area that does work for the Department of

Defense won a significant contract which considerably increased their revenue. It donated over $100,000 of that increase to an area non-profit organization that takes care of orphans.

Money is _____ just for you.

Define your personal philosophy about money.

_____

_____

_____

_____

_____

Maximizing money for yourself and others

A sage proverb states, "The wise person saves for the future, but the foolish person spends whatever they get." When it comes to money, the way to be wise is to be a saver. Four simple rules given by the late financier, J.P. Morgan, for saving money are a) start early. Today is the day to start your savings program; b) save a definite amount; c) save regularly and systematically; and d) employ your savings productively.[21]

Another wise but often underutilized key to wise money management is minimizing or eliminating debt, particularly consumer debt. One person quipped, "The only reason a great many American families don't own an elephant is that they have never been offered an elephant for a dollar down and easy weekly payments."[22] Seriously, the accumulation of personal financial debt has resulted in many families suffering hardship including loss of their homes and even bankruptcy. Debt has contributed to fractured or ended relationships. Buying and accumulating things, even if they are legitimate needs, with credit (money you really don't have) is a foolish _____ best to avoid.

KIRSTEN'S STORY

Nerdy, eccentric, and exceedingly intuitive, Kirsten lived for MMORPGs—massively multiplayer online role-playing games. Under the alias "Sicarius," she spent all of her waking hours aside from work living in these virtual worlds. She was particularly drawn to games about England in the Middle Ages and legendary Camelot.

While Kirsten was an expert gamer on the internet, she had no proficiency in the real world when it came to money. If she had it, actual or credit, she spent it. She dumped thousands of dollars into her gaming obsession. In no time, she had buried herself under a seemingly insurmountable mountain of debt. When her car was repossessed, Kirsten was living in a small apartment and dangerously close to becoming homeless.

That's when her older brother, Derek, intervened on his sister's behalf. Together they decided that they would have to agree in advance on anything Kirsten spent. That level of accountability was difficult for Kirsten, and eventually they had to add Derek to her bank account, so he could track Kirsten's expenditures.

It took over a year, but with her brother's help and love, Kirsten restructured her finances and her habits. She got a better paying job and reduced the time she spent gaming. In three years, Kirsten was totally out of debt, had started saving money—and now sees the experience as being essential. "Everything happens for a reason," she told Derek. "If I lose faith in that, then nothing in my life makes sense."

Questions for application:

1. What is your consumer debt story?

_____

_____

_____

_____

_____

2. What caused you to handle your debt that way—and how did you improve your situation?

_____

_____

_____

_____

_____

3. Are you currently able to save money? If so, how does it make you feel? If not, what else needs to happen so that you can begin building a savings account?

_____

_____

_____

_____

_____

Finally, a sound money management strategy is to utilize portions of your income or savings to _____ more money. In her book, *The Nuts and Bolts of Investing*, investment and securities advisor Carol Jones offered basic facts to both novice and seasoned investors to help them make good decisions with their money. When it came to handling money and investments, Carol saw the process as being much like a journey.

"Normally, you begin with a destination in mind, and then make a plan about how to get there ... You really can't begin unless you've set some goals and then developed a plan. Without this preparation, you might take profits or losses at the wrong times, lose track of your portfolio, or buy an inappropriate investment on the spur of the moment. Once you figure out your goals to clarify your investment objectives, you can then work your plan with the knowledge of how much money you have, what you want to put that money into, and why you are doing it."

As you consider how you can elevate your attitude by maximizing the money you have now, and will earn in the future, as a resource for yourself and a benefit to others, here is a collection of practical facts and tips from Carol's book.

1. Before investing, your current income must cover your basic living expenses, plus emergencies such as a broken furnace or car repairs. You must also have adequate insurance.

   a. By this standard, how are you doing covering your basic living expenses and possessing adequate insurance? If you have a shortfall, are you in any way mismanaging your income to contribute to that?

   _____

   _____

   _____

   _____

   _____

   b. What does your answer to Question A tell you about your attitude toward money? Explain.

   _____

   _____

   _____

   _____

   _____

2. Begin your investment journey by putting the maximum dollars allowed into a retirement savings plan. After that, you use whatever is left to build an investment portfolio.

    a. What is your view about having a retirement savings plan or an investment portfolio? Why do you feel that way?

_____

_____

_____

_____

_____

    b. What does your answer to Question A tell you about your attitude toward money? Explain.

_____

_____

_____

_____

_____

3. Shares of stock represent ownership capital in a corporation and are usually bought in 100-share lots (a standard number of trading units), although it is possible to buy as little as a single share of a stock.

    a. What is your view about buying stock shares? Why do you feel that way?

_____

_____

_____

_____

_____

b. What does your answer to Question A tell you about your attitude toward money? Explain.

_____

_____

_____

_____

_____

4. A bond is a fixed income investment in which you loan money to an entity for a defined period of time at a variable or fixed interest rate. Bonds are generally purchased in one- to five-thousand-dollar blocks.

a. What is your view about investing in bonds? Why do you feel that way?

_____

_____

_____

_____

_____

b. What does your answer to Question A tell you about your attitude toward money? Explain.

_____

_____

_____

_____

_____

5. Most *mutual funds*, holding companies where shareholders' funds are pooled and invested by a money manager, require much smaller minimum purchases; some will take as little as twenty-five dollars. Regular, small investments in a mutual fund may be a great way to start investing while minimizing risk. You simply want to make sure that the costs you pay your broker or investment advisor for small purchases are reasonable.

a. What is your view about investing in mutual funds? Why do you feel that way?

_____

_____

_____

_____

_____

b. What does your answer to Question A tell you about your attitude toward money? Explain.

_____

_____

_____

_____

_____

6. Investment *risk* refers to the likelihood that you will lose your money in that investment. Have a clear understanding of the risk involved before you make any investment decision. Investments whose values do not fluctuate carry the lowest degree of risk, but historically have the lowest rate of return over long periods of time. Other investments may be subject to large fluctuations in value. They come with a higher degree of risk of losing your money, but also have the chance to realize the highest returns.

a. Would you assess your mindset about taking investment risk as conservative, aggressive, or somewhere in between? Why do you feel that way?

_____

_____

_____

_____

_____

b. What does your answer to Question A tell you about your attitude toward money? Explain.

_____

_____

_____

_____

_____

Balancing risk and return is an essential part of building a portfolio. In general, a younger person with good earning power and some savings has time to weather riskier investments, while someone past retirement age usually cannot replace large financial losses and would be better served by conservative investments.

Write down your responses to the following questions to gauge your inclination to invest your money:

1. What standard of living do I have now?

_____

_____

_____

2. Do I want it to continue, and for how long?

_____

_____

_____

3. What are my retirement goals?

_____

_____

_____

4. Do I have children to educate or aging parents to support?

_____

_____

_____

5. How much time do I you have for my investments to produce the results I want, especially before I retire?

_____

_____

_____

_____

_____

6. Now that I've learned more, what kind of financial risks am I really willing to take?

_____

_____

_____

Once you've answered these questions, you can determine where to allocate your investment dollars and perhaps discuss these questions with a certified financial planner.[23]

Remember, money is a resource—so while your finances should never be the source of your identity, it can certainly be an _____ of your identity, shown in your mindset about how you use it.

In *Financial Healing from the Inside Out*, my longtime colleague, Dr. Amanda H. Goodson, and her co-author, Angela C. Preston, cite the importance of having a healthy relationship with money. "Virtually every major decision you make involves some consideration of the monetary consequences," they wrote. "What you do, where you live, and with whom you associate are all impacted by your mindset about money. Often, those attitudes and beliefs come from your childhood or cultural experiences that taint your perspective. Examining the source of our mindset allows you to discard thinking that no longer serves your purpose, allowing you to create a new set of attitudes and beliefs."

When you have the right attitude about money, the result is freedom. Goodson and Preston say it best. "Financial freedom may look different for each person, but freedom from finances generally means being free of all debt: no outstanding loans, no credit card debt (never carrying any balances forward and incurring added interest), and no mortgages. It means no payments to anyone for any reason. Financial freedom can also mean that you now have multiple revenue streams—savings and investments that allow enough flexibility for you to be able to retire to do what you want when you want and how often you want, where you choose to do it for however long you want to do it. Financial freedom is being able to enjoy a self-directed life where you get to call all the shots in terms of how, when, and where you spend your time. Financial freedom may also be the choice of living a frugal lifestyle rather than acting in an irresponsible manner, especially if failure to do so will put your financial freedom at risk."

They conclude, "True financial freedom shows that you have taken control of your finances."[24]

ADAM'S STORY

A military brat born in the Bronx, Adam's New York City upbringing was centered around his family. He said his mother had a very intimidating stare and was always firm but loving. When he was a kid, his no-nonsense grandmother used to tell him, "He who hangs out with the wolves learns how to howl." So, inspired by his father's military service, he joined the U.S. Army and served with the Special Forces, gaining a variety of specialties including electronic surveillance and animal training.

After he was honorably discharged, Adam didn't join security or law enforcement as many of his fellow soldiers did. Instead, he became a certified canine coach. Adam trained several service dogs of different breeds and sizes to help people with assorted disabilities as well as to help former military servicemen and women coping with trauma.

With his beloved Belgian Shepherd, Penelope, at his side, Adam shared how his chosen life's work is an extension of his identity. "I know I could've taken my service skill set and pursued any number of more lucrative professions, but I wanted to earn an honest living doing something to give back to families. I've taken care of my finances, remained free of debt, and can therefore control what I do in life." He added, "Besides, my grandmother was right. I love dogs, and I've learned to howl with the best of them."

Questions for application:

1. How has your family background influenced both what you do and how you see and manage your finances?

_____

_____

_____

_____

_____

2. In what ways is your use of money an extension of your identity?

_____

_____

_____

_____

_____

3. What was your first thought when you read, "Financial freedom is being able to enjoy a self-directed life where you get to call all the shots in terms of how, when, and where you spend your time." What does that tell you about your current attitude about money?

_____

_____

_____

_____

_____

As we elevate our attitudes about our confidence, emotional intelligence, and money, we are then positioned to be leaders in our society, our workplaces, and our homes.

It is an incredible responsibility, and our success is predicated on following the right example.

Attitude of Money **Fill-in-the-Blank Answer Key:**

difference	wisdom	create
self-centered	value	extension
wisely	never	
perceive	pitfall	

5

ATTITUDE OF A SUCCESSFUL LEADER

Look out for other people and put them first.

In his book, *The Spirit of Leadership: Cultivating the Attributes That Influence Human Action*, leadership consultant Dr. Myles Munroe defined leadership as "the capacity to influence others through inspiration, motivated by a passion, generated by a vision, produced by a conviction, and ignited by a purpose." Leadership expert John C. Maxwell simply said, "leadership is influence, nothing more, nothing less."

When the board of directors of a large food company was considering the selection of a new president, one of the directors worked out this questionnaire. Read each question slowly and carefully. Every one of them is telling when it comes to the _____ of a successful leader who looks out for others and puts them first.

1. Who of the possible candidates is the best known as a personality to the most company people?

2. Who is the most liked and trusted by them?

3. Who is held in the highest regard outside the organization...in public life and in the trade?

4. Who is the most warmly human when dealing with people?

5. Who has demonstrated the best capacity for selecting able people and the greatest willingness to delegate authority and responsibility?

6. Who will be apt to do the best job of keeping his or her desk and mind clear of day-to-day operating problems in order to have time to think in broader terms of tomorrow and next year?

7. Who does the boldest—yet soundest—thinking?

8. Who is most open-minded and willing to revise decisions when important new facts come to light?

9. Who inspires the best cooperation and exercises the best control and coordination without trespassing on responsibility once delegated?

10. Who is most self-possessed in all situations, best able to adjust to personalities and circumstances with tact and understanding?

11. Who can be depended upon to make the most of a promising new plan or idea?

12. Who can "take it" the best under a heavy load of responsibility?

13. Who is the best builder of the people?

14. Who is most likely, in good times and bad, to remember that the basic job of the president is to operate the business at a profit?[25]

ROSE'S STORY

Rose was a disciplined, overachieving business administration student with a fervent work ethic and a laser focus on her academic advancement and career goals to become a successful corporate executive. She had her life path completely mapped out.

Then came the night Rose was brutally victimized during a shooting at a boat party. She barely survived with her life, and the trauma she experienced completely altered her mindset. She became withdrawn, apathetic, and generally cold toward everyone, including family and friends with whom she had deep relationships. Rose also became very sarcastic. "I used to have ambition. I used to be passionate. Inspired. Alive. Now, I am mostly just hungry."

For a while, food (particularly anything spicy) became her primary coping mechanism, dramatically changing her physical appearance and harming her health. Thankfully, her friend, Peyton, wouldn't let Rose go. She patiently but determinedly worked Rose through her trauma and helped Rose find her path once more and discover who she had always been: a positive individual who was devoted to her vocational goals, as well as a loyal friend.

Today, Rose is a corporate president and chief executive officer in the Pacific Northwest, and she and Peyton volunteer to help other crime victims escape their trauma and find new life outside its confining walls. To Rose's joy, her employees and colleagues view her as a leader who is warmly human when dealing with others.

Questions for application:

1. How is dealing with others with warm humanity a vital leadership trait? Explain.

_____

_____

_____

_____

_____

2. Which one of the earlier 14 leadership attribute questions resonated most with you—and why?

_____

_____

_____

_____

_____

3. What setback or trauma have you had to overcome to become who you are right now? How did you do it?

_____

_____

_____

_____

_____

Helping others win

Mark Miller, the vice president of High Performance Leadership at Chick-Fil-A, elaborated on servant leadership in his book, *The Heart of Leadership: Becoming a Leader People Want to Follow.* He wrote, "Servant leadership is an approach contrary to conventional leadership in which the leader's focus is on himself and what he can accomplish and achieve. Rather, the focus is on those being served." While Miller said servant leaders do many of the same things other leaders do, such as cast vision and build teams, the big difference is their orientation and motivation. "They possess an _____ mindset. The servant leader constantly works to help others win."

I once hired a female leader who had a lot of potential to be a great executive. She possessed talent in decision making, change management, and team building. She had a big drive for excellence. She wanted to be the best and to help as much as possible, and she was on board with the vision that I had cast for the company. Her ceiling of advancement was high, so I set aside time to become a mentor to her.

We discussed improvement in areas such as people skills and in having overall wisdom when making executive decisions. The time I dedicated to her was taken from time that I could have been doing things for myself, but I decided to put her future first. She was a very open-minded mentee who took to heart everything she learned. Within three years, she had advanced in her career and currently serves as our vice president of operations.

Tell the story of when you set aside time and made the effort to help someone else win.

_____

_____

_____

_____

_____

Servant leadership also works because it _____ others—acknowledging their different roles, responsibilities, and strengths. As Miller put it, "It is not about who's in charge. It's about who is responsible for what, and how can I, as the leader, help people be successful."

A super guy who possessed the rare talents of negotiation and conflict resolution came into my circle when we sat on the same non-profit board. Immediately recognizing his gifting, I hired him to fulfill a few specific roles to help take my organization to another level, first as a consultant and later as a staff member. I acknowledged his strengths and put them to use in various ways— and he told me it was his confidence in my leadership philosophy that helped him to grow and be able to improve those around him.

In that philosophy, I allow people to fail and learn from their mistakes, all while knowing that I have their backs. It was something he had never seen in other leaders, and it allowed him to have a safe place to mature and allow his talents to flourish. It continues to be a joy to watch him work and grow.

What is the greatest takeaway value of being allowed to fail and learn from your mistakes?

_____

_____

_____

_____

_____

Leaders who are servants don't blame others. They own their actions and their outcomes. This speaks to _____ where leaders praise others on their team when they do well and take full responsibility for the good or bad outcomes of the team.

Ability Plus is an organization with many moving parts that is monitored by strict state rules. We are subject to an annual audit from the state that requires us to accept auditors who have different personalities and want things done in various formats. Therefore, we often have to go to our house managers and other staff during the audit period with demands that can bring great stress to our entire team.

In 2021, during our annual review from the state regarding the services we provide, we were cited in several areas, and the auditor went over all the improvements needed for our organization to be in full compliance. Instead of blaming my team for the problems at hand, I told the auditors that the issues were my responsibility as CEO and that we would address them and move to a positive status. I promised to personally oversee the process to the end. It's difficult to take responsibility instead of passing it on to others, but it's always best to be proactive rather than reactive.

1. Describe a time when you took responsibility for yourself and others when presented with a difficult challenge?

_____

_____

_____

_____

_____

2. How did this type of accountability help you to better understand your own strengths and weaknesses?

_____

_____

_____

_____

_____

Finally, servant leaders are men and women who see things *that could be*—and Miller pointed out that the future they see is always a _____ version of the present. "We believe we can make a difference; we think we can make the world, or at least our part of it, better," he said.

When I took over Ability Plus, the company was in big trouble from a financial, structural, and cultural viewpoint. As a servant leader, I addressed the team to let them know that we were going to be better in the future. I did not have all the answers or the resources, but I had the mindset to roll up my sleeves and get to work with a determination to motivate others to do the same. I told the staff that I would not ask them to do anything that I wasn't willing to do myself.

They saw me get up every day and stay in the fight with them. I told them often that I appreciated what they did. I told them we would learn as we went. We all leaned on each other's strengths—and we turned things around.

MALCOLM'S STORY

As a young detective, Malcolm was ambitious and serious. He had a desire to earn the respect of his colleagues and prove his competence. He didn't hesitate to use any method, including unorthodox ones, to be resourceful and reveal different avenues of investigation. As long as it was legal and ethical, Malcolm delved into any lead that could aid him in solving his cases.

So, when Malcolm later opened his own private investigation firm, he infused his team with his ideas and mindset. Often, he came against skepticism and even outright opposition to some of his techniques. But he incessantly trained and encouraged his investigators to both think and act outside the box, understanding that resolving and wrapping up their assignments to their clients' satisfaction was paramount.

Today, Malcolm's servant leadership has produced a firm that has a nearly 100 percent ratio of solved cases that resulted in a criminal conviction. As to the keys that make him an effective servant leader, Malcolm said, "I read a lot, almost anything and everything. I make an effort to use any knowledge I attain and express my opinions, even at the risk of being wrong at times." He added, "Spiritually, I pray and meditate. Emotionally, I challenge myself to be open, honest, and available."

Questions for application:

1. The positive outcomes of Malcolm's investigative methods helped him to see "what could be" as he worked with the team at his firm. What helps you see "what could be" as a professional? Explain.

_____

_____

_____

_____

_____

2. What do you need to change about yourself so that you can see the future as a better version of the present?

_____

_____

_____

_____

_____

3. Which one of Malcolm's quoted personal keys to effective servant leadership do you want to develop more in your life? Why?

_____

_____

_____

_____

_____

Foundational attitudes of great leadership

Leaders think differently about themselves. That is what distinguishes them from followers. I've identified seven attitudes that are foundational to great leadership. Some of these attitudes may be more present in the personality of one leader than another, but each of these attitudes can be strengthened.

Whether they naturally possess these qualities or not, great leaders are _____ to consistently develop each one of these attitudes to elevate their unique leadership roles.

1. A great leader has exemplary character

Miller wrote of leadership being like an iceberg: 10 percent above the waterline and about 90 percent below. The part above the water indicates leadership skills, but the rest below represents leadership character. "If you want to predict people's ultimate success as leaders," Miller said, "evaluate not their skills but their leadership character."

It is of utmost importance that leaders are trustworthy. They should be known to live with honesty and integrity. Great leaders "walk the talk," earning the _____ to have responsibility for others as they do. Servant leadership builds trust simply because we trust leaders whose motives are centered around others.

True authority is born out of the respect and trustworthiness shown by great leaders. In addition, servant leaders should be people of _____ responsibility and, when needed, monetary sacrifice. While working as CEO of Ability Plus, I received an offer to take a job that would've tripled my annual salary and provided other attractive benefits. It was an incredible opportunity, but after prayer and counsel from other trusted people, I decided that purpose, not money, should be the criteria to take the position.

When we chase our purpose and passion, money will follow. Money is not the endgame. I turned down the offer to remain in my purpose and passion at Ability Plus, knowing that when you walk in your purpose, you are walking in you.

a. Which attribute of exemplary character is your strongest? Why?

_____

_____

_____

_____

_____

b. Which attribute of exemplary character is your weakest? How can you begin to improve it?

_____

_____

_____

_____

_____

2. A great leader is enthusiastic about their work or cause as well as about their role as a leader

It's undeniable that people will respond more openly to a person of passion and dedication. Leaders need to be a source of inspiration and a _____ toward the required action or cause. Although the responsibilities and roles of each one of these leaders may be different, they need to be part of the team, unafraid to roll up their sleeves and get dirty. Tom Landry, former head coach of the National Football League's Dallas Cowboys and one of the finest leaders professional sports has ever known, once said, "Leadership is a matter of having people look at you and gain confidence, seeing how you react."[26]

Early in my career as a pastor, my first church was a young ministry that was growing at a constant rate. That meant our initial facility was not sufficient for us to have the programs and outreaches we wanted for the community. So, I found an old warehouse that had a lot of potential but was quite run down. It needed a ton of work, but I was enthusiastic about what we could do with the building.

As an engineer, I mentally drew up my plans for it and communicated them to my church leadership team. We got the property, remodeled it, and used it for the next three years. The highlight was the summer youth program that it allowed us to facilitate. After moving into the building, one of my elders revealed that, in reality, the leadership team didn't see anything that I saw in my mind, but my enthusiasm caused them to follow my recommendation to acquire the building.

ALY'S STORY

Sensible and straightforward, Aly was never afraid to call people out: a personality trait that equipped her well to be an attorney. Aly enthusiastically buried herself in her work. This had some incredibly positive outcomes for the community she served. She helped uncover a huge corporate conspiracy that put away that company's unsavory owner and president. But being a lawyer was all Aly knew.

It wasn't until her longtime friend and old college roommate, Olivia, introduced her to an organization advocating for the rights of disenfranchised workers—some of whom had been taken advantage of by the very company leader Aly prosecuted—that Aly found a cause that she could become as passionate about as her vocation. As she got involved, Aly ended up helping many of those workers and their families to find better housing and high-paying employment opportunities. In addition, Aly became more understanding of and flexible about how she lived her own life.

Today, Aly is seen as a leader not only for her abilities in the courtroom, but for how she interacts with and inspires her fellow attorneys. "You have to be happy with yourself first of all. That's the most important thing. Despite my success professionally, I wasn't actually happy with me until I truly got involved with Olivia giving back to others. That has made me a leader worth following."

Questions for application:

1. What are you most enthusiastic about in your workplace? Why?

    _____

    _____

    _____

    _____

    _____

2. What cause outside of your workplace are you most enthusiastic about, and why?

    _____

    _____

    _____

    _____

    _____

3. How can you combine both of those enthusiasms to further develop yourself as a leader?

    _____

    _____

    _____

    _____

    _____

3. A great leader is confident

In order to set direction, leaders need to be confident as individuals and in their leadership role. Such a person inspires confidence in others and draws out the trust of the team to complete the task well. A leader who conveys confidence toward the proposed objective brings out the _____ in all those around them. Dr. John Haggai, the great outreach executive who raised up leaders worldwide, once said, "Leadership is the discipline of deliberately exerting special influence within a group to move it towards goals of beneficial permanence that fulfills the group's real needs."[27]

When I started doing leadership consulting through Vision Excellence Company, I didn't know anyone who had started such a company. Yet I had a vision in my heart for it. Within three months of moving forward, two doors of opportunity opened up to consult with two different organizations. I didn't have all the know-how I needed, but I did know that I would succeed. I was confident in myself and my vision. That humble beginning has developed into a team providing seminars, training, and coaching in a dozen different strategic areas to help individuals and organizations lead, innovate, and grow.

How have you delivered confidence in such a way that it brought out the best in those around you? Tell the story.

_____

_____

_____

_____

_____

4. **A great leader functions in an orderly and purposeful manner during times of uncertainty**

People look to their leaders during transition or turmoil. During the Nazi occupation of his country in World War II, King Christian X of Denmark noticed a Nazi flag flying over a Danish public building. He immediately called the German commandant, demanding that the flag be taken down at once. The commandant refused.

"Then a soldier will go and take it down." said the king.

"He will be shot," threatened the commandant.

"I think not," replied the king, "for I shall be the soldier."

Within minutes, the flag was taken down.[28]

Others find reassurance and security when their leaders portray a _____ demeanor in trial or difficulty. As a member of the advisory board for the business school at Alabama A&M University, I was tasked with serving on a committee to assist the dean, faculty, and staff to achieve international accreditation. There were many requirements to get the certification, and we could not be distracted with others' opinions about how hard it was going to be to achieve that status.

It took two years, but we got it done. That international accreditation serves to protect the interests of the university's students, their parents, the institution, and potential employers by ensuring that the educational programs offered have attained a level that meets or exceeds standards that were developed by experts in their fields.

a. Describe a time you kept a positive demeanor during a trial or difficulty?

_____

_____

_____

_____

_____

b. What was the outcome?

_____

_____

_____

_____

_____

5. **A great leader is tolerant of ambiguity and remains calm, composed, and steadfast to the main purpose**

Storms, emotions, and crises come and go—and great leaders take these as part of the journey and keeps a cool head in the midst of them. It's been said that the first responsibility of a leader is to _____ reality. Leaders need to have a good picture of what is really going on around them, and they need to help others take an honest look at this reality.[29]

During the 2021 audit of Ability Plus that I mentioned earlier, the state representative asked to see our procedures for tracking the behaviors of our clients. These behaviors can include acting out, a response to a medical treatment, or a deterioration in their overall condition. We had recorded this information using a form the state representative didn't like or understand—so we had no other choice than to change our form and tracking procedures to fit the representative's request. We had to take the information we had, put it into the new form, and then make sure the procedures read the way the state wanted. This took weeks, and to say the least, was not appealing to our team. But we reminded one another to stay calm under pressure.

ROBERT'S STORY

A former college jock turned social worker, Robert is a very protective person. He shows concern for everyone he cares about. He also possesses a strong sense of justice that energizes the cases he oversees, sometimes without adequate concern about the dangers inherent in those situations.

Yet Robert and his colleagues see this as both a necessary risk and a strength. Robert has an uncanny ability to remain focused and composed regardless of the circumstances of the adults and children he advocates for. This positions Robert to define the reality they are facing, and that enables them to communicate their plight to him and articulate possible solutions. In the office, Robert often brings his perspective to cases that his fellow social workers are dealing with, empowering them to more honestly and accurately serve their clients.

"I guess something I took from my time as an athlete was the reality that, at any time, I could've suffered an injury that would've jeopardized my season, my career, or maybe even my long-term health. Yet I couldn't let that effect or diminish my performance on the field or on the court," Robert said. "Defining my reality and staying cool was rooted within me then, and I've just carried that forward into my professional life."

Questions for application:

1. In general, how do you feel you respond to storms, emotions, or crises? Explain.

_____

_____

_____

_____

_____

2. What can you draw from in your past experiences to help you become cooler under pressure?

_____

_____

_____

_____

_____

3. How would you define your reality right now in your workplace? What do you like (or not like) about that answer?

_____

_____

_____

_____

_____

6. A great leader is able to think analytically and stay focused on the goal

Not only do great leaders view a situation as a whole, but they are able to break it down into subparts for closer inspection. Not only is the end goal in view, but it can be broken down into manageable steps so that progress can be made. Leadership is the ability to put the plans into _____, and to accomplish the specified objectives through the skillful management of people, time, and tangible resources. A good leader is one who is able to motivate people; one who is capable of making good decisions, even under pressure or in conditions of uncertainty; one who can guide people through actions as well as words.[30]

When I launched Vision Excellence Company, I had a goal of becoming more involved in the community because I wanted to increase my influence among senior leaders in northern Alabama. After receiving advice on how to proceed with this goal, I developed a plan to achieve it that focused on leading with purpose and making a difference in the community. It couldn't be done all at once, so I had to exercise patience along the way as each step required a different level of maturity.

First, I established a relationship and partnership with the local Chamber of Commerce. Second, I started to support community charities by attending several of their monthly and annual events. Third, I served on the boards of six different non-profit organizations in the region. This led to me being asked to be part of several key groups of influence, helping me to learn and grow from other leaders throughout the area.

In all, it took four years to achieve my goal, and I not only met my expectations, but I exceeded them.

a. On a scale of 1-10 (with 10 being the highest), how do you rate your ability to think analytically?

_____

b. Why did you give yourself that score?

_____

_____

_____

_____

_____

7. A great leader is committed to excellence

Second best does not lead to success. Great leaders not only maintain high standards, but they are _____ in raising the bar in order to achieve excellence in all areas. Someone once said, "Do not follow where the path may lead, go instead where there is no path and leave a trail."[31]

The two leaders who raised the bar and left a trail in my life as a leader and as a person also happened to be two of my amazing mentors. The first, mentioned at the very beginning of this workbook, was Dr. David Green, Jr. He was dean of the science and math department at Kettering University (formerly GMI Engineering & Management Institute) in Michigan before he retired. He chose me from a slate of students in Alabama to go to the General Motors Institute to further my original career as an engineer.

He mentored me all five of the years I was there, and even when I wanted to quit, he challenged me to stay. He said he knew there was greatness inside of me—something that I kind of felt back then but wasn't convinced was totally real. I didn't think that I could live up to it. Dr. Green didn't give me an out. He forced me to buckle down and do what I had to do. His tenacious guidance propelled me to my engineering career and prepared me to transition into what I'm doing today.

The second was Dr. Maurice K. Wright. My pastor for over 25 years and my spiritual father, he was a sounding board every time I needed one. One of the wisest men I have ever known, he constantly encouraged me, saying that I was special and telling me that God had a special calling on my life that I couldn't run from.

"You can't deny it," he said. "You have to embrace it." He always told me to welcome the opportunities that came my way and to never feel like I didn't deserve them, because I did.

Both of these men, leaders committed to excellence, were individuals who supported me and spoke into me so that I could be positioned to succeed by fulfilling my destiny as a leader.

1. Who would you identify as the leader or mentor who has most impacted your life? Tell their story.

   _____

   _____

   _____

   _____

   _____

2. Who could you begin to mentor as a leader? Write their name here—and describe how you feel you can best propel them to excellence.

   _____

   _____

   _____

   _____

   _____

"In order to be a leader, a man must have followers—and to have followers, a man must have their confidence. Hence the supreme quality of a leader is unquestionably integrity. Without it, no real success is possible, no matter whether it is on a section gang, on a football field, in an army, or in an office. If a man's associates find him guilty of phoniness, if they find that he lacks forthright integrity, he will fail. His teachings and actions must square with each other. The first great need, therefore, is integrity and high purpose."[32]

That quote, spoken by President Dwight D. Eisenhower, rings true for leaders of all genders and from all walks of life. All of us need to be successful leaders—and that elevated attitude requires us to look out for other people and put them first. In order to put others first, we need to be part of a team. Each one of us accomplishes more when we're in it together.

No leader does anything on their own. They don't take credit on their own. They don't turn the company around on their own. They don't make progress on their own. It takes a team with everybody doing their part and operating in their expertise—and that's what we'll talk about next.

Attitude of a Successful Leader **Fill-in-the-Blank Answer Key:**

qualities	diligent	positive
others-first	right	define
honors	fiscal	practice
accountability	motivator	proactive
better	best	

Notes

_____

_____

_____

_____

_____

_____

_____

_____

_____

_____

_____

_____

_____

_____

_____

_____

_____

_____

_____

_____

_____

_____

6

ATTITUDE OF TEAMWORK

All devoted to one. One devoted to all.
That is what makes up an effective team.

I first learned how to build an effective cohesive leadership team not in business, but as a pastor. When my wife and I launched Emmanuel The Connection Church in 1996, we immediately recognized that we needed a team to succeed in our vision of saving and empowering people. The mission was too big for a couple of people to achieve. More than that, we did not want to be just another building on the corner with a name on it. We wanted our church to make a real difference in the Huntsville community.

We had all these ideas of what we wanted to do, but we had to plan, discuss, and agree upon who was going to do what, when they were going to do it, and how they were going to get it done. We had to be on the same page. It was a challenge because we had some people who had left other church organizations to be a part of ours, and each one came to us with different titles, roles, and abilities. We had to help them understand our vision and how they fit into making it come to pass.

We started by _____ the team about talents to find out their strengths. Next, we laid out the specific outreaches we wanted to do, and we assessed where everyone fit best. We took it one step at a time and asked everybody to be a team player.

It took a year-and-a-half to get where we needed to be, but we did it—and our church indeed had a phenomenal impact in the community because we worked as a team.

1. Share the story of your most recent experience serving on a team. This could be at work, at church, or at home.

   _____

   _____

   _____

   _____

   _____

2. What did you most enjoy about the experience...and why? What did you least enjoy about it... and why?

   _____

   _____

   _____

   _____

   _____

3. What did the team achieve—and did it meet, exceed, or fall short of its goal?

   _____

   _____

   _____

   _____

   _____

Essential elements of teamwork

Bees teach us something about teamwork. On a warm day about half the bees in a hive stay inside beating their wings while the other half go out to gather pollen and nectar. Because of the beating wings, the temperature inside the hive is about 10 degrees cooler than outside. The bees rotate duties and the bees that cool the hive one day are honey gatherers the next.[33]

There is no substitute for having an Attitude of Teamwork. First, **support of one another** is _____ in teamwork. The entire group of people who make up the team are not supported by one person, but by each other. They are stronger together operating on the same plan. Teamwork is the key to achieving our dreams and, from an organizational perspective, to accomplishing our mission and vision.

Second, it is very important that each person on the team **knows their role.** Just as the many cultures of the world have their great followers and leaders, each team has great _____, some who are destined to succeed individually, and others who are purposed to be leaders and will take their team to higher places. Whatever their role, each member of the team relies on the other.

FRASER'S STORY

As a soldier and as a landlord, Fraser is charming, amiable, and a natural leader. His strongly developed social intelligence, dogged stubbornness, and profound sense of duty and honor combine with his sense of humor and utter devotion to his family to make Fraser who he is: someone who won't turn away from any fight or responsibility that he perceives as his own.

Yet whether it was in the combat areas where he was deployed or on the properties and with the tenants he now oversees, team building and management has proven to be absolutely essential to Fraser's success and influence. He facilitates this not only through a weekly, structured one-hour meeting with his entire property management team, but via in person, one-on-one lunches with each manager in which he listens, advises, and encourages each man and woman so they are fully responsible for their own growth and success. These interactions allow Fraser's team to know their roles yet be fully enabled and supported.

Fraser shared his foundational belief for his leadership style. "Every day every person has a choice between right and wrong, between love and hate," he said. "It was during my military service that I first realized that I had become a leader, and understanding our responsibility to choose—and choose well—is the key to achieving what's best for our team and our clients."

Questions for application:

1. What do you like about Fraser's leadership style as described above? Is there anything you would change or add?

_____

_____

_____

_____

_____

2. Describe how you feel you best support others at the workplace.

_____
_____
_____
_____
_____

3. What are your workplace roles and responsibilities? Does anything need to change to help you understand them better?

_____
_____
_____
_____
_____

Unity is the last essential element of teamwork. Unity is the glue that keeps everyone moving in the same direction for a _____ cause. Without unity, talents will find themselves in an unproductive state. "Snowflakes are one of nature's most fragile things," someone once said, "but just look at what they can do when they stick together."[34]

The biggest challenge to unity is making sure each person understands their goals and their roles in achieving those goals, then ensuring that every team member puts aside their individual egos. It is not about how I want to do it. It is about what needs to be done for the goal to be achieved. Many times, people have their own unique takes on how to get there, but there is a right way defined by our organizational values and culture.

Recognizing individuality and talents to maximize them, then translating them in the team to the mission and purpose, is the key. They have to see how their individual goals are wrapped up in the overall goal so they can still achieve what they want, but to the benefit of the entire team.

1. Describe a time you had to set aside what you wanted for the betterment of the entire group.

   _____

   _____

   _____

   _____

   _____

2. How did that decision affect your ego—and develop your appreciation of the importance of unity?

   _____

   _____

   _____

   _____

   _____

   In the end, no organization can be _____ without unity. I know that's a bold statement, but it is made after years of experience. When unification is absent in a team, individual talents and egos begin to war against each other. The project, process, and plans are ultimately destroyed, and the organization dies.

   I recall a statewide alliance of leaders that wanted to share in community projects and meet the needs of those less fortunate. But because of their lack of unity from a structural and organizational position, they failed, even after several attempts at trying to right the ship. They couldn't decide who was going to lead, and they did not have a clear mission or vision statement. In addition, they never pinpointed their overall "why." They knew they needed to exist, but they never got to their purpose.

CATRINA'S STORY

Compassionate and sensible, Catrina is a police officer in North Carolina who naturally takes charge and keeps a cool head. Intuitively averse to taking orders without first questioning them, Catrina's attitude and words sometimes get her into trouble, but that's par for the course for her as a thoroughly independent woman.

When Catrina was asked by her commander to represent the department on a team of leaders designed to increase and enhance overall community service in the northwestern Carolinas, she was initially skeptical. She was aware that her inclination toward personal autonomy could be a detriment to her success on the team. However, as she began experiencing the group's training, empowerment, and collaboration, she thrived, and so did the team's efforts. Each year, additional leaders from around the state joined the cause, and they had a positive impact on thousands of people. Catrina grew under leadership that had a clear vision and mission and precise objectives. Most of all, there was uncompromising unity, and that unity prompted growth and results.

"My experiences have taught me to cherish the present because tomorrow might not ever come to pass," Catrina said as she participated in one of the group's community outreaches, a "Hope Fest" that delivered free dental and medical care to low-income families and individuals. "The work we're doing together, here in the moment, is a testament to the unity we've built."

Questions for application:

1. How are a clear vision and mission and precise objectives essential to maintaining unity in a team setting?

   _____

   _____

   _____

   _____

   _____

2. What is the essential difference between the statewide alliance of leaders that failed and the group Catrina got involved with that is succeeding? Explain your answer.

   _____

   _____

   _____

   _____

   _____

3. How do you think a person's natural independence can be channeled to become an asset in a group setting?

_____

_____

_____

_____

_____

Organizational effectiveness = team cohesiveness

The word "team" is often overused in the sense that we usually refer to any group with more than one person as a team. But a true team is not just two or more people, but a group that is moving in the same _____ to accomplish a goal or mission.

This necessitates cohesiveness—and there are three ways, when evaluating an organization, that team cohesiveness will bring about overall effectiveness.

1. **Building the team.** An organization needs a team that works well together. Functional, cross-functional, and self-managing teams are the three different types of teams found within an organization, and each team has its own specific goals and objectives.

    Functional teams are the traditional teams that generally have a lot of oversight and are in the same discipline: they are all engineers or accountants.

    Cross-functional teams have members from several disciplines, possibly including someone from marketing or human resources, working to achieve a particular goal.

    Self-managing teams come up with new ideas on their own. Management has approved this team's work in advance, and its members are not afraid to explore, act, and then present their results to executive leadership.

    By resolving conflicts, brainstorming new solutions, initializing innovation, and providing a supportive and encouraging environment for all of these teams, you will improve the _____ of individual team members and the organization as a whole. One of the greatest ways to do this is through team building activities. As you provide ample opportunities for the members of your team to interact with and get to know one another, they learn to trust and depend on each other and care for one another.

What type of team (functional, cross-functional, or self-managing) do you feel most comfortable being a part of...and why?

_____

_____

_____

_____

_____

2. **Establishing a goal pyramid.** To create an efficient system for achieving goals and making viable progress in a timely manner, do what ancient architects did: create an unshakable structure with at least three levels—company goals, team goals, and individual goals.

   This goal pyramid starts with your ultimate vision at the very top, followed by team goals at the middle level, and individual tasks and objectives on the bottom. It is a fantastic tool to foster unity, provide transparency, and keep your employees from getting sidetracked from the predetermined road to success. Setting clear _____ on each level is a phenomenal way to measure progress, keep the operation's big-picture goals at the forefront of everyone's minds, and map out a way for every team member to contribute to the larger vision of the organization.

   The goal pyramid is created with the executive team looking at the vision and mission statement from one-year, five-year, and 10-year perspectives, and then building company goals for each team and drilling down to establish team goals and what each person needs to do to accomplish those goals. The pyramid is first presented to the team in a group "lunch and learn" setting where they can get fired up, excited, and motivated. It is then shared in detail with team leaders and, through them, to each individual.

   This is exactly the type of work we do with our clients through Vision Excellence Company.

   Of the three general levels of the goal pyramid—company goals, team goals, and individual goals—which tier do you think is most prone to weakness? Explain your answer.

_____

_____

_____

_____

_____

3. **Fostering transparency.** There is no better way to accomplish flawless team cohesion than by leading your crew with complete transparency. Business management expert and author Patrick Lencioni refers to this as "getting naked" in his book about client loyalty. It is vital to take the time to enlighten every member on goals, procedures, and policies while setting crystal clear objectives so that each member knows how they are expected to contribute to the overall success of the company.

   Leading with complete transparency provides everyone with a clear understanding of what they're working _____ and how they can support the greater good of the organization. Never punish anyone for being transparent. In fact, you want to provide tips and guidance to encourage transparency and reward people for being transparent.

   Integrity is required to establish and solidify transparency. Lencioni wrote that integrity is healthy when it is whole, consistent, and complete—meaning that operations, strategy, and culture all fit together and make sense. When operations are doing things in an honest way to support the overall strategic plan that encompasses the established culture, organizational health is achieved. Transparency mandates telling the truth, even if it hurts or costs you something. When you start compromising and not telling the truth, it becomes easier to do, and it infects the culture. Owning up to mistakes might be tough, but it is always the right thing to do.

RICHARD'S STORY

The son of a Presbyterian minister, Richard's journey into ecumenical leadership representing a number of different Christian churches was an unusual one. Studious yet relaxed with a mischievous sense of humor, his early career was focused on education, serving as one of the youngest professors on the staff of various college campuses. He taught history and, with a scholar's insatiable curiosity, he was passionate about the subject. It came as no surprise that it was a research project that reintroduced him to his religious roots and informed his decision to leave teaching and go into full-time ministry as an ecclesiastical speaker and bridge builder.

The biggest challenge Richard has faced since taking on that leadership role has been overcoming a culture of secretiveness within church organizations. He's found that it is extremely hard to get ecumenical leaders, particularly reverends and pastors, to be honest and transparent with one another. The setting aside of fierce territorialism and an acceptance of an "agree to disagree" mentality regarding doctrinal issues—not the potential exposure of personl improprieties—are constant hurdles Richard strives to overcome as he works with clergy.

"Words have consequences," he says. "I've also discovered that integrity is the state of being honest and undivided, and such integrity is absolutely required if the Christian church is to be truly relevant in this day and age."

Questions for application:

1. Do Richard's revelations about secretiveness in church culture echo anything clandestine you've observed at your workplace? Why or why not?

_____

_____

_____

_____

_____

2. Do you feel comfortable or uncomfortable when you consider, as Patrick Lencioni wrote, "getting naked" in how you interact and work with your colleagues and/or customers? Elaborate on why you feel that way.

_____

_____

_____

_____

_____

3. What incident frst came to mind when you read, "Transparency mandates telling the truth, even if it hurts or costs you something." Share the story and its outcome.

_____

_____

_____

_____

_____

Five key behaviors of effective teamwork

A *Chicago Tribune* article once told the story of Chad Kreuter, a reserve catcher for the Chicago White Sox, who severely dislocated and fractured his left shoulder on a play at home plate. He underwent surgery, and the White Sox placed him on the 60-day disabled list. That's exactly the kind of thing that can make a backup player feel even less like a part of the team.

But quite the opposite happened. Chad's teammates had a strong liking for him, so each one put Chad's uniform number 12 on his ball cap to show support. This gesture made Chad feel like he was a part of the team even though he couldn't play. Later in the season, after Chad was recovered and able to play once again, he showed his appreciation by putting the uniform number of each of his teammates, every one of them, on his cap.[35]

All devoted to one. One devoted to all. That is what makes up an effective team—and that type of devotion to one another is created and nurtured by five key behaviors.

1. **Building trust.** Dictionary.com defines a steward as someone who manages another's property or financial affairs; one who administers anything as the agent of another or others. Implicit with their role is that they can be fully trusted. In a business setting, a steward is defined as someone who uses resources in a systematic, accountable way and is concerned about the sustainability of the organization. This steward manages cash flow, employee relations, innovation, and other parts of the business for the betterment of the organization, its employees and customers, and any other stakeholders.

   Successful stewardship begins by building trust within your team. There are two types of trust. Predictive trust involves knowing how someone on your team will _____ in a given situation. For example, my consulting firm worked for an insurance company that had an agent who was directed to build positive relationships and interactions with customers who had strong issues and concerns regarding their policies. We predicted that the agent would lose his cool when the customer pushed hard against him—and we were right. He was placed in a coaching program to train him on how to better work with people. He corrected his behavior, improved, and has done well ever since.

   Then there is vulnerability-based trust where team members are completely transparent and _____ with one another. When teams have this kind of trust, teammates can genuinely say to each other, "I need help," "I messed up," "I can learn from you," or "You are better at that." While working with a government contracting company and conducting Emotional Intelligence training with its staff, it was revealed that people there felt very safe to share their vulnerabilities with their teammates. They were not afraid of being disrespected or marginalized when asking for help or admitting that they had a problem. In the midst of the training, many others around the table started talking about when they had issues, and their teammates and leaders were very receptive. Everyone was on the same page, and there was clear camaraderie in place that improved the culture.

Which type of trust (predictive or vulnerability-based) is most important to you... and why?

_____

_____

_____

_____

_____

Of course, at the heart of vulnerability is a _____ to abandon self-pride and fear and sacrifice ego for the good of the team. There was a time when I was working with a large nonprofit organization where the executive director showed great vulnerability-based trust. The organization needed a change in culture and mindset to go to the next level, and he had to move past his ego and admit that how he had been leading the organization was not effective. He admitted to being a little off-center when it came to his vision for the future and where the industry was headed. He showed greater care for the business than for his pride, and he allowed others to help him correct his errors and create the culture change.

The main thing that prevents new team members from building trust is the Fundamental Attribution Error. First identified by social psychologist Lee Ross in 1977, this error speaks to our tendency as human beings to attribute the negative or frustrating behaviors of our colleagues to their intentions and personalities while attributing our own negative or frustrating behaviors to environmental factors.

I saw this happen one time when a mid-level manager at a particular company exhibited very negative behaviors that were consistently witnessed by her teammates and other peers. The manager was judgmental toward others in the company, even those outside of her department. She took punitive actions when she felt the behavior of others was not in sync with company policies or culture. She made statements that suggested others behaved in a way intended to harm or even destroy the company. Yet when this manager was confronted about her own behaviors, she always attributed them to the systems and conditions she was placed in by management. It wasn't until she received coaching that she recognized what was going on with her and how she affected others. She corrected herself and is still with the company.

In the end, building trust is the first and most important behavior listed because it provides the foundation for all of the others.

a. Tell the story of a time you attributed the negative or frustrating behaviors of others to their intentions and personalities while attributing your own negative or frustrating behaviors to environmental factors.

_____

_____

_____

_____

_____

b. How was trust undermined in this situation? What would you do differently today?

_____

_____

_____

_____

_____

2. **Mastering conflict.** No one likes taking sides in a conflict, much less being in one themselves. But conflict is not only essential to personal development and to being effective as a member of an organizational team, it is a normal part of life. That's good because, contrary to popular wisdom, conflict is *not* a bad thing for a team. In fact, when trust is present in a team, conflict becomes nothing else but the _____ of the truth.

I remember working with leaders of an organization where one of the executives had a different idea on how maintenance should carry out its roles in the company. Most of the leaders viewed the maintenance department as being overwhelmed with open tickets to fix everyday problems and felt it needed a separate person to be in charge of long-term preventive maintenance issues. But the one executive felt strongly that the department was simply not managing its time properly and could be more aware and proactive about those long-range issues.

A detailed SWOT analysis (a study undertaken by an organization to identify its internal strengths and weaknesses, as well as its external opportunities and threats) and an on-the-ground evaluation was conducted. It was readily confirmed that the maintenance department did not have enough time to perform as required but could make improvements to better manage the time it had. The conflict resulted in the truth being exposed and the situation was rectified.

On the other hand, conflict without trust becomes politics: an attempt to manipulate others in order to win an argument regardless of the truth. One company had a supervisor who felt it was his personal duty to be in conflict with everyone. He used his position and title to manipulate people to war against one another just to get his point across. Those who worked for him only followed his direction because they were afraid of getting fired. He was eventually let go because his conflict was not healthy for the company. In the end, politicizing is almost always bad and divisive.

1. On a scale of 1-10 (with 10 being the highest), how do you rate your own ability to deal with conflict in team settings?

    _____

2. Why did you give yourself that score?

    _____

    _____

    _____

    _____

    _____

Naturally, disagreement during conflict brings with it a level of _____ even among the most trusting of team members. Overcoming the tendency to run from that discomfort is one of the most important requirements for any team leader, calling to mind the familiar adage, "No pain, no gain."

At one organization, there was a team member who was loyal but fed up with her supervisor's manipulative tactics. She was a stellar leader, had endured other politics in the office, and remained solid in her work performance, but she was still planning to leave the company out of frustration. Thankfully, other leadership assured her the executive's behavior would no longer be tolerated, he was removed from the company, and she chose to remain. Ultimately, she was promoted to that former executive's position, and the company is thriving under her leadership. None of it was easy or comfortable, but the result was great gain for everyone.

Avoiding discomfort in conflict only transfers greater quantities of mistrust into more groups of people throughout the organization. It is also true that different people and varying cultures participate in conflict in different ways. In many African American cultures, individuals may raise their voice levels during conversation, which may seem to some to be yelling. But it is actually a normal way they communicate during conflict. It may appear to be hostile and rude when they are in fact showing the highest level of respect for one another. The seemingly aggressive physical gesturing that may accompany such a conversation is not an indication of anger or mistrust, but of conviction of thought. Two people who are engaged in something important and who trust and care for one another should feel free to disagree, sometimes passionately.

Have you ever had to defend or explain your cultural context during a conflict? If so, tell the story and its outcome. If not, what does the previous paragraph teach you that you can use during future conflicts?

_____

_____

_____

_____

_____

This conflict continuum is vital, yet it necessitates the employment of two conflict tools, particularly when there is a strong cultural aversion to the discomfort conflict brings.

Mining for conflict allows effective team leaders to establish an obligation to show dissent, knowing that if they don't, conversations that should be happening in the open will instead occur in isolated pockets and behind closed doors to the detriment of the team. While it is natural to desire consensus, the more productive approach is to get more people to speak and share their ideas so that ultimately, as Lencioni says, you "avoid the destructive hallway conversations that inevitably result when people are reluctant to engage in direct, productive debate."

Real-time permission enables team members to coach one another instead of retreating from healthy debate. When people engaged in conflict are becoming uncomfortable with the level of discord, they should be reminded that what they are doing is necessary so they will have the confidence to continue. Once the meeting has ended, it is helpful to remind those participants that the conflict they just experienced was good for the team and not something to avoid.

Cohesive teams must take a few minutes to ensure that everyone _____ each other. At the end of one executive board meeting that saw much conflict, the team decided to move forward with an updated strategic plan. Everyone around the table was asked individually if they had an issue or any questions about the new additions. Those were addressed and everyone was supportive of the plan.

SOPHIE'S STORY

Sophie is a study in seeming opposites. Possessing bachelor's degrees in world history and mechanical engineering, she likes to build things and work through problems logically. Yet she is also imaginative and creative, and her freehand abilities with pencil and paint place her in high demand as a commissioned artist.

Yet Sophie uses her understanding and acceptance of these conflicting skill sets to help others recognize and embrace the totality of their own gifts, and see and affirm the talents of others, as a team leader at the power plant where she works. This awareness among the colleagues she coaches has enabled their teams to mine for conflict more effectively and engage in upbeat, constructive debate to determine solutions to the problems they address as a team. As a result, the overall performance of the power plant has improved, and customers have experienced improved service.

"I'm a history student. I like watching history be made," Sophie said. "I feel the outcomes of our work as a team will leave a positive legacy not just for the communities we serve, but for each one of us as individuals who have learned to appreciate what every person brings to the table."

Questions for application:

1. What are two personal and/or professional skills you possess that seem to be opposites? Describe each one.

_____

_____

_____

_____

_____

2. How do these skills work together to shape how you think and operate in your workplace?

_____

_____

_____

_____

_____

3. What change do you recommend that could help you and your colleagues ensure that they understand one another as you participate in your teams?

_____

_____

_____

_____

_____

3. **Achieving commitment.** It's been said, "You must get involved to have an impact. No one is impressed with the won-lost record of the referee."[36]

Conflict is vital—for a team cannot achieve commitment without it. Good conflict brings out what needs to be done, addresses the why, who, and what, and leads to a goal that the team can commit to and achieve. The only way to prevent bad communication is to arrive at specific agreements. The problem with communication is many times we think we have done it well when we actually did not do a good job of it at all. Clear communication that is both properly heard and understood is important.

At the same time, waiting for consensus in communication before taking action can lead to mediocrity and frustration. One company had a situation where they needed to change how payroll was handled and when they would pay team members. A new vendor had all the tools and support the company needed to make the changes, but not everyone was on board, and some were even fearful they might not get paid on time. So, leadership had the payroll company come in and do a demonstration of the capabilities of the new system and how it would execute and deploy the needed changes. After proper vetting, leadership decided to go forward even though one of the executives in human resources was against it. A beta test was done as a trial with a sample of team members, it worked well, and it brought consensus to the group.

It's only when people see true commitment that they will be _____ to embrace accountability.

Describe a time in the workplace when you thought you did a good job communicating but actually didn't—and how the situation was resolved.

_____

_____

_____

_____

_____

4. **Embracing accountability.** To hold someone accountable is to care about them enough to risk having them _____ you for pointing out their deficiencies—and on a team, peer-to-peer accountability is the primary and most effective source of being answerable and responsible to one another.

   I hold myself accountable to those I lead. When there is a new project, initiative, or program that we have said we are going to do, I ask my team to hold my feet to the fire on quality, care, and delivery time of the outcomes. I developed a program of rewarding team members who did this by recognizing a winner via video each week. This was difficult to do with my very hectic schedule, but I made it happen, and the team benefited from the program.

   On cohesive teams, peers confront one another without having to involve leadership. This avoids distractions and politics. Two mid-level managers of an influential organization had a disagreement concerning the process and the depth of information that should be given to those outside of their cross-function strategy group. One felt that everything discussed should be shared in its entirety. The other believed that only a summary of highlights was necessary. Without going to leadership, they came up with a solution both liked. A general summary was to be shared, with the agreement that if more info was requested, it would be given.

   Do you find it easier to hold yourself accountable or challenge others with their accountability? Explain your answer.

_____

_____

_____

_____

_____

As part of embracing accountability, team leaders must overcome the "wuss" factor. They cannot _____ out when confronting team members on their behavior. I saw this play itself out at a large organization that had a close executive team. An executive had to confront another peer who was not taking accountability for the actions of his team. He had team members who were lagging in their duties, causing his department and others within the company to suffer. The executive told the peer about the issue and challenged him to correct things before the situation escalated and the CEO got involved.

It was hard to do. The executive and his peer had worked together for years and were friends, but in this case, the overall health of the company and its teams was more important than their personal friendship and had to be addressed. In the end, the peer could not deny the problem and truly wanted to do his best for everyone. Even though it was an uncomfortable situation, the person who was doing the offending behavior recognized it and corrected it—and no harm was done to the friendship.

LAUREN'S STORY

The last thing Lauren wanted to do was confront her supervisor, César, about what she knew was happening at the print shop where she was employed as a press operator. As she oversaw the machines and monitored systems for irregularities during orders, Lauren identified staff negligence that caused needless machine malfunctions and costly halts in production. A primary responsibility of her role was to make sure that safety guidelines were being met for all press machines, including workspace cleanliness. Yet revealing the oversights and laxity she observed would take Lauren well outside her comfort zone.

Beneath her quiet demeanor was an extremely determined and strong personality, and Lauren drew on that inner characteristic as she met with César. Somewhat to her surprise, her supervisor not only listened carefully to her report and concerns, but he followed up her accusations with a personal internal investigation that proved Lauren's findings.

"A huge part of me didn't want to say anything," Lauren later admitted to her best friend, Brianna. "But I knew I had to take responsibility as a leader and get over my hesitance." Six months later, Lauren received a pay raise and a letter of commendation from the corporate headquarters.

Questions for application:

1. Do you relate to Lauren's story in how you view confrontation at the workplace? Why or why not?

_____

_____

_____

_____

_____

2. When have you had to draw from an inner characteristic of your identity to face a challenge? Tell the story.

_____

_____

_____

_____

_____

3. Why is being accountable, even when it is uncomfortable, so important in a team setting?

_____

_____

_____

_____

It is important to distinguish between the main forms of accountability.

Measurable accountability is easier with leaders because there are no gray areas. It is not just based on someone's judgment and theory. Measured accountability is described in specific terms (such as amount and duration) that can be easily seen.

At the same time, *behavioral* accountability is more important than measurable accountability because behavioral problems almost always precede performance downturn. Most people's actions don't just show up out of thin air. The behaviors exist, but they may not have yet manifested themselves. Therefore, it is very important to address behaviors in their _____ when proper leadership can gear the individual in the right direction. It should be looked at as a strategic planning objective and addressed as soon as possible. If it isn't, the behaviors will either stay hidden or they will manifest themselves in even worse ways.

Think of a current team that you are a part of at your workplace. Which type of accountability (measurable or behavioral) is most important to it...and why?

_____

_____

_____

_____

_____

5. **Focusing on results.** When we work together while doing what we are supposed to do individually, then we can grow as a team and get the results we expect from our work. As each person takes responsibility for their own roles, growth and outcomes will occur. Ultimately, the whole point of building greater trust, conflict, commitment, and accountability is one thing: the achievement of results. No matter how good a team feels about itself or its outcomes, if _____ are not achieved, then it is not a good team.

Cohesive teams work together to achieve a goal despite conflict and trials. They embrace the need to commit themselves to learn from one another and build the trust that will enable them to cross the finish line together. On the other hand, a non-cohesive team is only concerned with individual members looking good whether the team achieves its goal or not. Being seen as the MVP (most valuable player) of a team is great, but what really matters is winning the game. This is one reason why goals are shared across the entire team—and the only way for a team to maximize its output toward these goals is to establish the same priorities and row in the same direction.

When consulting with a large gym company that had multiple locations, it was discovered that most of the gyms' managers were leading from their own direction and doing their own thing. If an employee went from one gym to another one in the company, they discovered that things were being done in a totally different way. My consulting team decided to visit all seven gyms, posing as customers interested in getting a membership, when we were really covertly analyzing each gym's internal processes. After a detailed study of each location, we brought all the managers together for a "best practices" seminar. The managers were not even aware that there was no continuity in processes and services between gyms. They corrected this, and it resulted in better customer experience and improved revenues.

What workplace result are you most fulfilled from being a part of? Tell the story.

_____

_____

_____

_____

_____

An Attitude of Teamwork requires everyone to let go of ego and selfish ambition and come together with others to achieve excellence and success. When it comes to our performance, motivational speaker and self-improvement author, Brian Tracy, talks about having a positive mental attitude, and he believes that approximately 85 percent of our performance is based on our attitude. Positive mental attitude is essential to understanding ourselves in concert with understanding others to obtain maximum outcome.

Attitude of Teamwork **Fill-in-the-Blank Answer Key:**

teaching	objectives	understands
critical	toward	positioned
players	react	blame
common	honest	wimp
healthy	willingness	infancy
direction	pursuit	goals
performance	discomfort	

DAILY DEVOTION
TO ELEVATING YOUR ATTITUDE

Viktor Frankl, a survivor of Nazi concentration camps in World War II, eloquently and poignantly stated, "Everything can be taken from a man but one thing: To choose one's attitude in any given set of circumstances—to choose one's way."[37]

If you want to lead, if you want to grow, and if you want to be better, it all starts with your mindset. If you want to be rich, you can't have a poverty mentality. If you want to be the head, you can't stay the tail. Your attitude puts you in another place and carries you to an optimum state of optimism, hard work, and patience.

Therefore, you must intentionally strive each day to have an attitude that will enable you to achieve anything you want in life and to positively impact the people around you. It is not just going to happen. You must wake up every morning with a mindset that there are no bad days—only good days that will have challenges to overcome—challenges that will make you better and stronger.

Every day, I read something positive, listen to something positive, and try to find something positive in everything I see and do. You have to train your mind every single day. This is not a lifestyle that denies the realities of life or the negatives around you. Rather, it is a daily devotion in which you tool your mind so that when the challenges come (and they will), you will be able to respond in a proactive and productive manner that reflects the different attitudes I have detailed throughout this book. No matter what is going on or how things appear, when we elevate our attitude, we will not have bad days.

Join me in pursuing life—choosing *your* way—with the proper attitude to succeed.

You'll never be the same.

Read or listen to something positive, according to each chapter's theme, over the next two weeks. Then, for each chapter's topic, write down what you learned below.

_____

_____

_____

_____

_____

_____

_____

_____

_____

_____

ENDNOTES

1   Today in the Word, June 11, 1992. Taken from www.sermonillustrations.com

2   Reader's Digest, January, 1992. Taken from www.sermonillustrations.com

3   Bits & Pieces, May 28, 1992, p. 15. Taken from www.sermonillustrations.com

4   Richard Conniff, "Racing with the Wind," *National Geographic*, September 1997, p. 52-67.

5   Konosuke Matsushita, founder of the PHP Institute, Inc., as quoted in Bits & Pieces, August 20, 1992, pp. 22-23. Taken from www.sermonillustrations.com

6   Bits & Pieces, May, 1991, p. 15. Taken from www.sermonillustrations.com

7   Bits & Pieces, January 7, 1993, pp. 11-14. Taken from www.sermonillustrations.com

8   www.researchgate.net/publication/276002060_Rosenberg_Self-Esteem_Scale_Greek_Validation _on_Student_Sample

9   www.toppractices.com/blog/the-importance-of-self-improvement-and-personal-growth.cfm

10 Harvard Business School Online. www.online.hbs.edu/blog/post/business-skills-for-engineers

11 Adapted from www.makemeanalyst.com/characteristics-of-scientific-method/

12 J. Stowell, Fan The Flame, Moody, 1986, p. 44. Taken from www.sermonillustrations.com

13 Jan Riggenbach, "Midwest Gardening," *Daily Herald*, May 8, 1994. Contemporary Illustrations for Preachers, Teachers, and Writers, Craig Brian Larson, p. 26.

14 Bits & Pieces, August 22, 1991. Taken from www.sermonillustrations.com

15 Dr. Gary Collins, in Homemade, July, 1985. Taken from www.sermonillustrations.com

16 Christopher News Notes, August, 1993. Taken from www.sermonillustrations.com

17 "Towering Courage and Trust," p. 64. 500 Illustrations: Stories from Life for Preaching & Teaching, G. Curtis Jones and Paul H. Jones, Abingdon Press, 1998.

18 www.betterme.world/articles/examples-of-emotional-intelligence/

19 www.quora.com/What-are-some-real-life-examples-showing-emotional-intelligence

20 Ecclesiastes 5:10-12. THE HOLY BIBLE, NEW INTERNATIONAL VERSION®. Copyright© 1973, 1978, 1984, 2011 by Biblica, Inc.™. Used by permission of Zondervan.

21 George Fooshee, Homemade, Vol. 11, No. 4, (April 1987). Taken from www.sermonillustrations.com

22 Source unknown. Taken from www.sermonillustrations.com

23 Carol Jones, *The Nuts and Bolts of Investing*. Publisher, Adam Colwell's WriteWorks, March 4, 2019.

24 Angela C. Preston and Dr. Amanda H. Goodson, *Financial; Healing from the Inside Out*. Independently published, Amanda Goodson Global, February 27, 2019.

25 Bits & Pieces, May 26, 1994, pp. 18-20. Taken from www.sermonillustrations.com

26 Today In The Word, August,1989, p. 30. Taken from www.sermonillustrations.com

27 Dr. John Haggai, "Lead On!" Taken from www.sermonillustrations.com

28 Today in the Word, August, 1991, p. 13. Taken from www.sermonillustrations.com

29 Richard J. Mouw, *Uncommon Decency*, p. 117. Taken from www.sermonillustrations.com

30 George Barna, *How to Find Your Church*, pp. 104-105. Taken from www.sermonillustrations.com

31 Source unknown. Taken from www.sermonillustrations.com

32 Dwight D. Eisenhower, Bits & Pieces, September 15, 1994, p. 4. Taken from www.sermonillustrations.com

33 Bits & Pieces, September 17, 1992, p. 19-20. Taken from www.sermonillustrations.com

34 Vesta M. Kelly. Taken from www.sermonillustrations.com

35 Bill Jauss, "Catcher and Sox Both Seriously Hurt," *Chicago Tribune*, July 20, 1996, Sec. 3, p. 10; Steve Rosenbloom, "Hit and Run," *Chicago Tribune*, September 29, 1996, Sec. 3, p. 1.

36 John H. Holcomb, The Militant Moderate (Rafter). Taken from www.sermonillustrations.com

37 Taken from www.sermonillustrations.com